Fundamentals of Operating Systems

Fifth Edition

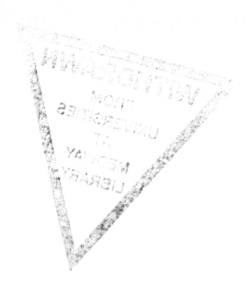

Fundamentals of Operating Systems

A. M. Lister

University of Queensland

R. D. Eager

University of Kent at Canterbury

Fifth Edition

Springer Science+Business Media, LLC

First edition 1975
Reprinted 1977, 1978
Second edition 1979
Reprinted 1980 (twice), 1981 (four times), 1983 (three times)
Third edition 1984
Reprinted 1984, 1985, 1986
Fourth edition 1988
Reprinted 1989 (twice), 1990, 1991, 1992
Fifth edition 1993

ISBN 978-1-4757-2254-3   ISBN 978-1-4757-2252-9 (eBook)
DOI 10.1007/978-1-4757-2252-9

Library of Congress Cataloging-in-Publication Data
is available.

Contents

to my parents

Preface to the First Edition

An operating system is probably the most important part of the body of software which goes with any modern computer system. Its importance is reflected in the large amount of manpower usually invested in its construction, and in the mystique by which it is often surrounded. To the non-expert, the design and construction of operating systems has often appeared an activity impenetrable to those who do not practise it. I hope this book will go some way toward dispelling the mystique, and encourage a greater general understanding of the principles on which operating systems are constructed.

The material in the book is based on a course of lectures I have given for the past few years to undergraduate students of computer science. The book is therefore a suitable introduction to operating systems for students who have a basic grounding in computer science, or for people who have worked with computers for some time. Ideally the reader should have a knowledge of programming and be familiar with general machine architecture, common data structures such as lists and trees, and the functions of system software such as compilers, loaders and editors. It will also be helpful if he or she has had some experience of using a large operating system, seeing it, as it were, from the outside.

The first two chapters of the book define the functions of an operating system and describe some common operating system characteristics. Chapter 3 establishes the process as a basic concept in the discussion of the concurrent activities which go on inside an operating system, and describes how processes communicate with each other. The rest of the book then describes the construction of an operating system from the bottom up, starting at the interface with the machine hardware and ending at the interface with the user. By the end of the book the system which has been constructed is seen to possess the features demanded at the beginning.

Throughout the book I have tried to show how each stage in the construction of an operating system naturally follows on the previous ones, and have emphasised the logical structure of the system as a whole. I have done this for two reasons. The first is pedagogical: my experience indicates that students gain a better understanding of complex material if it is presented in a coherent manner. The second is frankly polemic: this is the way I believe operating systems should be built. Attention to structure and logical dependence are the best means we have of building operating systems which are easy to understand, easy to maintain, and relatively error free. Finally, I would like to thank the many friends and colleagues who have helped in the writing of this book. In particular I would like to thank David Lyons, who has been a fertile source of ideas and comment; and David Howarth, who made valuable comments on an earlier draft. Thanks are also due to Colin Strutt, Morris Sloman, John Forecast, Ron Bushell and Bill Hart, who have made constructive suggestions for improving the text.

ANDREW LISTER

Preface to the Second Edition

Any book on computer science suffers from the fact that its subject matter is undergoing rapid change, both technological and conceptual. A book on operating systems is no exception: the hardware on which systems run is being revolutionised by the large scale integration of components, and ideas about what operating systems should do are being modified by changing user requirements and expectations. Although this book is about 'fundamentals', which can be expected to be less volatile than other topics, it would be foolish to ignore the developments which have occurred in the four years since publication.

Consequently I have amended the text in three main ways for this edition. First, there is an additional chapter on reliability, a topic whose importance has increased dramatically as reliance on computer systems has grown in many areas of life. Secondly, the references to real-life operating systems have been updated to include systems which have come into use since the first edition, and references to the literature have been similarly updated. Thirdly, I have altered the presentation of certain topics so as better to reflect current ideas, and have expanded the conclusion to indicate what developments can be expected in the future.

Other changes in the text have been motivated by feedback from readers of the first edition. Here I owe a great debt to my students, who have had the perception to point out errors, and the good sense to expose inadequate exposition. Any improvements in this respect are due largely to them, though any remaining inadequacies are, of course, my own.

A.L.

Preface to the Third Edition

Almost a decade after publication it is reassuring to know that the 'fundamentals' of the title remain essentially the same. However, as the systems of the early 1970s fade into distant memory I have found it necessary to update the text by reference to their successors. I have also taken the opportunity to introduce one or two new topics, and to improve the presentation of several others. In this latter respect I am indebted to Morris Sloman and Dirk Vermeir for their valuable suggestions, and, as ever, to my students.

A.L.

Preface to the Fourth Edition

I feel honoured to have been asked to update this book for its fourth edition. I have used all of the earlier editions as part of my own teaching of operating systems, and am glad to have had the opportunity to revise this excellent text to reflect recent developments. The main changes are in the chapter on filing systems, but there are many other areas where new systems and techniques have merited mention. Finally, I would like to thank the person who first taught me about operating systems many years ago when I was a student – Andrew Lister.

Bob Eager

Preface to the Fifth Edition

It is now nearly twenty years since the first edition of this book was published. Much has changed, yet much has remained the same.

Because true fundamentals do not alter, there have been no radical revisions to the text. However, we have taken the opportunity to update a number of areas, with the inclusion of more examples drawn from modern systems. We have deleted mention of some systems which have long disappeared, but references to important early systems still remain. We have also updated and expanded the list of references, and hope that this will direct the reader towards further areas of interest.

BOB EAGER AND ANDREW LISTER

1 Introduction

In this chapter, and the next, we attempt to answer the questions:

- What is an operating system?
- What does it do?
- Why do we need one?

By answering these questions we hope to give the reader an idea of what we are trying to achieve when we discuss, in later chapters, how operating systems are constructed.

We start by examining the broad purpose of an operating system, and by classifying various types of operating system currently in existence.

Broadly speaking an operating system performs two main functions, as follows.

(1) Resource sharing

An operating system must share the computer's resources among a number of simultaneous users. The aim is to increase the availability of the computer to its users, and at the same time to maximise the utilisation of such resources as processors, memory, and the input/output devices. The importance of resource utilisation depends on the cost of the resources concerned – the continuing decline in hardware costs has led to decreasing emphasis on resource utilisation, to the extent that many microcomputers are dedicated to a single function and never shared at all. Large computers, however, are still expensive enough to warrant considerable effort in sharing their resources. Increasingly, even microcomputers are used for multiple functions, although they may have but a single user; in such cases, resource sharing is still a relevant issue.

(2) Provision of a virtual machine

The second major operating system function is the transformation of a raw piece of hardware into a machine which is more easily used. This may be looked on as presenting the user with a *virtual machine* whose characteristics are different from, but more tractable than, those of the underlying physical machine. Some areas in which the virtual machine often differs from the underlying real machine are as follows:

1

(a) Input/Output (I/O)

The I/O capabilities of the basic hardware may be extremely complex and require sophisticated programming in order to utilise them. An operating system will relieve the user of the burden of understanding this complexity, and will present a virtual machine with I/O capabilities that are much simpler to use, though equally powerful.

(b) Memory

Many operating systems present a virtual machine whose memory differs in size from that of the underlying real machine. For example, an operating system may use secondary memory (probably in the form of magnetic disks) to give the illusion of a larger main memory; alternatively, it may partition the main memory among users so that each user sees a virtual machine whose memory is smaller than that of the real machine. These two techniques may even be combined for different users of the same machine.

(c) Filing system

Most virtual machines include a filing system for the long term storage of programs and data. The filing system is usually based on the disk storage of the real machine, but the operating system allows the user to access the stored information by giving a symbolic name rather than by providing details of its physical location on the storage medium. The virtual machine also allows some structure to be imposed on the stored information.

(d) Protection and error handling

Since most large computer systems are shared by a number of users, it is essential that each user be protected against the effects of error or malice in others. Even in small systems, it is often necessary to protect users against themselves. Computers vary considerably in the degree of protection provided by the basic hardware, and the operating system must build on this to provide a virtual machine in which users cannot adversely affect either each other or the integrity of the system.

(e) Program interaction

A virtual machine may provide facilities for user programs to interact as they run, so that, for example, the output from one program is used as input to another.

(f) Program control

A virtual machine provides the user with a means of manipulating programs and data within the computer system. The user is presented with a human-computer interface which makes it possible to convey what the virtual machine is required to do – for example, the compilation and execution of a certain program, the amalgamation of two sets of data held in the filing system, and so on. This interface may take the form of a command language, or a graphical (pointing) system.

In either case, the interface is at a much higher level, and is much easier to use, than the basic machine code instructions executable by the physical machine.

The precise nature of a virtual machine will depend on the application in which it is to be used. For example, the characteristics required for an airline seat reservation system will differ from those required for the control of scientific experiments, or for a desktop computer. Clearly, the operating system design must be strongly influenced by the type of use for which the machine is intended. Unfortunately it is often the case with 'general purpose machines' that the type of use cannot easily be identified; a common criticism of many systems is that, in attempting to be all things to all individuals, they end up being totally satisfactory to no-one. In the next section we shall examine various types of system and identify some of their characteristics.

1.1 Types of operating system

(1) Single user systems

Single user systems, as their name implies, provide a virtual machine for only one user at a time. They are appropriate for computers which are dedicated to a single function, or which are so inexpensive as to make sharing not worthwhile. Most microcomputer operating systems (for example, MS-DOS (Microsoft, 1988), which runs on around 100 million personal computers) are of the single user type. Single user systems generally provide a simple virtual machine which facilitates the running of a variety of software packages (for example, word processing or spreadsheet) as well as allowing users to develop and execute programs of their own. The major emphasis is on the provision of an easily used command language, a simple file system, and I/O facilities for keyboard, display, disk and printer. It should be noted that some more recent single user systems are capable of carrying out more than one task concurrently for the one user; in this case the single user system supports more than one virtual machine. Examples of such systems include OS/2 (Deitel and Kogan, 1992) and Windows NT (Custer, 1993).

(2) Process control

Process control generally implies the control by computer of an industrial process, such as the refining of oil or the manufacture of machine tools. It can be extended to include such things as environmental control in a space capsule or the monitoring of a patient's condition in a hospital. The common feature of all these applications is *feedback*; that is, the computer receives input from the controlled process, computes a response which will maintain its stability, and initiates the mechanism for giving it. If the input, for example, signifies a dangerous rise in temperature, then the response may well be to open a valve in order to increase the flow of coolant. Clearly there is a critical time within which the response must be given if the process is to remain in equilibrium, let alone safe! The main function of the operating system in process control is to provide maximum reliability with the minimum of operator intervention, and to 'fail safe' in the event of any hardware malfunctions.

(3) File interrogation systems

The distinguishing feature of these systems is a large set of data, or *database*, which can be interrogated for information. The response to information requests must occur within a short time (typically less than a minute), and the database must be capable of being modified as information is updated. Examples are management information systems, where the database consists of information on company performance, and medical information systems, in which the database is a set of patients' records. The user (company manager or doctor) expects to be able to access information without any knowledge of how the database is organised, either in terms of software structure or hardware storage devices. Hence the operating system must make interrogation facilities available without involving the user in details of implementation.

It is now more usual for file interrogation facilities to be added as an extra 'layer' on top of a general purpose operating system. This approach reduces the costs to the operating system vendor of supporting different variants of the software.

(4) Transaction processing

Transaction processing systems are characterised by a database which is frequently modified, perhaps several times a second. Typical applications are in airline seat reservations and banking. In the former the database contains information on seat availability, and is modified each time a seat is booked; in the latter it consists of details of accounts, which are updated for every credit and debit. The major constraint in transaction processing is the requirement to keep the database up to date; clearly the system is useless if transactions are made using incorrect data. Further problems arise in dealing with simultaneous transactions on the same datum (for example two travel agents trying to book the same seat), and with time constraints (the banking system may be connected directly to cash dispensers which are in use by impatient customers). The individual user should of course be unaware of these problems, and the operating system must resolve them so that (where appropriate) the individual has the impression of being the sole user of the system.

As with file interrogation systems, it is now fairly common for transaction processing systems to be added as an additional 'layer' on a general purpose operating system.

(5) *General purpose systems*

General purpose operating systems are employed on computers characterised by a large number of users performing a wide variety of tasks. Such systems are designed to handle a continuous flow of work in the form of jobs to be run on the computer. Each job performs a specific task for a particular user (for example, analysis of survey data, solution of differential equations, calculation of monthly payroll) and typically consists of running one or more programs. In a simple case, say that of survey analysis, the job may be no more than the running of an already compiled program with a particular set of data. More complicated jobs may involve modifying a program by use of an editor, compiling it, and finally running it. Because of the variety of jobs which may be submitted, the system must be able to support a large number of utility programs such as compilers for various languages, assemblers, editors, debugging packages, word processors, and a file system for long term storage of information. The system must also be able to handle the wide variety of peripherals which may be required (for example, terminal, bar code reader, document reader, impact printer, laser printer, graph plotter, magnetic tapes and disks, optical disks). The provision and control of these facilities, together with the organisation of the flow of work, are the broad functions of a general purpose operating system.

General purpose systems are often classified into two groups: (1) *batch*, and (2) *multi-access*. The chief characteristic of a batch system is that once a job enters the computer the user has no further contact with the job until it has been completed. A couple of decades ago, the job would have been punched on cards or stored on magnetic tape, and then passed to an operator for submission to the machine; when the job was complete the operator would have dispatched the printed output back to the user. Occasionally jobs would have been submitted from input devices situated at some distance from the central installation, and the output would have been printed at the same remote site. This would have been done by using a data transmission line between the central and remote sites, and was known as *remote job entry* (RJE). It would have been quite likely that several outlying sites would have been connected to the same central site, with the operating system ensuring that output was returned to the site from which the corresponding input was received. It is now more common for the user to submit a job from a terminal which is connected (either directly or indirectly) to the main computer, and to receive the output back on that terminal with the possibility of printing part or all of it at some later time. In neither a straightforward batch system nor a system with remotely submitted jobs is there any opportunity for a user to interact with the job while it is running.

In a multi-access (or *interactive*) system, on the other hand, a user may run one or more programs by typing on a terminal, and may use the terminal to monitor and control the running of these programs. The user may for example correct the syntax errors reported by a compiler, or supply data which are dependent on the results so far received. The operating system shares the computing resources among the various users so that it appears as if each user has exclusive use of the entire machine.

Many operating systems combine both batch and multi-access modes of operation; this is particularly true where batch jobs are submitted from a terminal. Because of the advantages of interaction, the multi-access mode tends to be used for activities such as program development and document preparation, while batch mode is used only for routine non-interactive tasks such as payroll and stock inventory, or for jobs that take a particularly long time to run.

Many of the systems described above may be implemented on a single computer, or on a number of connected computers. In the latter case the separate computers may share the workload equally, or each computer may be dedicated to servicing only one particular aspect of it. For example, one computer may operate in a fairly general fashion (handling I/O, scheduling work, and so on) while the other performs all work requiring intensive numeric processing. The computers may be located in the same room, possibly sharing memory and other resources, or they may be located at some distance from each other and communicate by means of data transmission lines. In such distributed systems the operating system must coordinate the activities of each computer, and ensure that the appropriate information flows between them as required.

1.2 System structure

It can fairly be said that many existing systems display very little logical structure at all. This sad fact may be attributed to three factors: first, many current systems were designed at a time when the principles of operating system construction were far less clear than they are now; second, the common technique of using large numbers of people to write complex software seldom results in a 'clean' product; and third, the previously mentioned desire for a system to be all things to all people often leads to the *ad hoc* attachment of new features well after the initial design stage. It is also the case that constraints imposed by peculiarities of hardware may often cause a well structured design to become blurred in implementation. However, we can reasonably hope that these constraints will become fewer as hardware design is modified to meet the needs of operating system construction.

There are a number of different ways in which operating systems may be structured. Three common approaches are described below.

(1) Monolithic

As already stated, most early operating systems (and some more recent ones) have no real structure. The operating system exists merely as a large program consisting of a set of procedures; there is no restriction on which procedures may be called by any other procedure, and little attempt is made to restrict the scope of system data. Such systems can be a maintenance nightmare, since modification of one procedure can cause problems in apparently unrelated parts of the system. It has been known for such systems to reach a point where the number of bugs is constant; any attempt to fix n problems introduces n new ones in exchange.

(2) Layered

Another way of structuring a system is to divide it into modules which are fitted together in layers; each layer provides a set of functions which are dependent only on the layers below it. Generally, the lowest layers are those which are the most critical in terms of reliability, power and performance.

The advantage of this structure is that the modular approach decreases the dependencies between different components of the system, reducing unwanted interactions.

Only a few real life operating systems have actually exhibited this rather neat structure. Notable research examples include T.H.E. (Dijkstra, 1968), and RC-4000 (Hansen, 1970). In the commercial world, there have been VME for the ICL 2900 series (Keedy, 1976; Huxtable and Pinkerton, 1977) and VMS for the DEC VAX and Alpha systems (Goldenberg *et al.*, 1991).

Modern processor designs often include facilities which ease the inclusion of layering; these include the ICL 2900 (Buckle, 1978), the Intel 80486 (Intel, 1990) and the DEC Alpha (Sites, 1993).

(3) Client-server

Another approach is once again to divide the operating system into modules, each providing some set of functions. However, instead of being arranged in layers, the modules are treated more or less as equals. They communicate not by calling procedures within each other, but by sending *messages* via a central message handler. Messages can flow in both directions, allowing results to be returned via a similar route.

The module sending the original message is known as a *client*, and the module receiving it (and providing the requested service) is known as a *server*. The status of a given module is not always the same; a server may be requested to perform some service which necessitates its sending a request to yet another module; it thus temporarily acts as a client.

This structure offers the same advantages as the layered approach, but with increased isolation and reduced dependency between modules (to the extent that the client and the server may well run on separate processors or even separate systems). The amount of critical code is also reduced. The most important component is of course the central one which provides message handling and other basic facilities; this is often known as a *microkernel*.

One example of a client-server system is Windows NT (Custer, 1993).

1.3 The 'paper' operating system

The majority of this book will be devoted to general purpose systems. However, several of the problems discussed also arise in other systems, and we shall indicate the relevance of our discussion to other systems wherever appropriate.

In order to study the way in which a general purpose system is constructed we shall build a 'paper' operating system; that is, we shall develop a hypothetical system on paper, in order to illustrate the principles involved. It will be our aim to develop this system in a logical manner, in that each stage of development will follow naturally from the previous one. This will be a layered system, and the direction of construction will be from the inside outwards, or 'bottom up', so that starting from a nucleus we shall add layers for memory management, I/O handling, file access, and so on.

As the development of our paper operating system proceeds we shall compare it with existing systems, and relate the techniques that we use to those employed elsewhere. In this way we shall keep our operating system firmly rooted in current practice, while using it as a vehicle for conveying the principles of operating system construction.

2 Functions and Characteristics of an Operating System

In this chapter we discuss in more detail the functions which we expect an operating system to perform, and isolate some of the characteristics it must exhibit in order to do so.

2.1 Operating system functions

We take as our starting point the raw machine – the basic computer hardware consisting of the central processor, memory, and various peripherals. (We defer until later consideration computers with more than one central processor.) In the absence of any software aids, the operation of loading and running a user program must be performed entirely under human control. Computer systems without such aids are difficult to imagine these days, although they were once quite common; thus we will take a somewhat historical example of a computer with a batch system using punched cards (or some similar medium) for input and a printer for output. Such systems do still exist, although they are very much in the minority. For each job, the operator had to perform a tedious sequence of tasks something like this

(1) place the source program cards in the card reader (or other input device)

(2) initiate a program to read in the cards

(3) initiate a compiler to compile the source program

(4) place the data cards, if any, in the card reader

(5) initiate execution of the compiled program

(6) remove results from the printer

The speed of the machine was obviously dependent on the rate at which the operator could press buttons and feed the peripherals, and this kind of system was therefore very much limited by the capabilities of that operator.

An obvious first improvement was to make the machine carry out automatically, without operator intervention, the sequence of steps necessary to read in, compile, load and execute one or more programs. The operator's role was thus reduced to loading cards at one end of the machine and tearing off paper at the other, and throughput was consequently increased. Of course one rarely gets something for nothing, and the price paid for increased speed was the dedication of part of the machine resources (some memory and some processor time) to a program which could perform the necessary job sequencing operations. Since all jobs did not necessarily require the same sequencing operations (some jobs, for example, might not need compilation) the control program needed to infer from one or more *control cards* precisely which operations were to be performed in any particular case. In other words, the control program had to be capable of interpreting a *job control language*. Furthermore, the errors which inevitably occurred in some jobs could not be allowed to affect jobs later in the sequence, and so the control program had to be responsible for handling errors in some rational fashion. Control programs with these features were in fact embryonic operating systems.

A system of this type was clearly limited by the speed at which it could perform input and output, and the next stage in improving efficiency was to reduce this dependency. This was first achieved by the technique of *off-lining*, whereby all output and input was performed to and from magnetic tape. The tasks of converting card input (or indeed input from other sources such as punched paper tape) to magnetic tape, and converting magnetic tape output to printed output (or punched paper tape) were relegated to a satellite computer of lower power and cost. The transfer of magnetic tapes between satellite and main computers was by hand. Off-lining systems, notably the IBM Fortran Monitor System, ran successfully from the late 1950s into the mid 1960s (there is an interesting modern parallel in the use of personal computers as 'front ends' to larger systems).

Off-lining reduced dependency by ensuring that all I/O was performed on magnetic tape, which was at the time the fastest cheaply available medium. The price paid was the addition to the embryonic operating system of a set of routines for coding and packing on magnetic tape data eventually destined for some other peripheral (and conversely for input). It should also be noted that because magnetic tape is essentially a serial medium there was no notion of scheduling jobs to run in any order other than that in which they were presented to the system.

In order to eliminate I/O dependency rather than merely reduce it, techniques were employed whereby I/O could be overlapped with processing. This was made possible with the aid of two hardware features – the *channel* and the *interrupt* – which are now in almost universal use. A channel is a device which controls one or more peripherals, performing data transfers between the peripherals and memory quite independently of the central processor. An interrupt is a signal which transfers control of the central processor to some fixed location, while at the same time storing the previous value of the program counter. Thus the program being executed at the time of the interrupt is temporarily abandoned, but can be resumed later at the point where it was *interrupted*. An interrupt from a channel acts as a signal to indicate that a data transfer has been completed. Hence it is possible for the central processor to initiate a peripheral transfer, to continue processing while the channel controls the transfer, and to receive notification by means of an interrupt when the transfer is complete. (The reader who wishes to learn more about channels and interrupt hardware is referred to any text on computer architecture, such as Baron and Higbie, 1992.)

Using channels and interrupts, it became possible to read in jobs onto some suitable storage medium (usually disk, since disk storage had by this time become generally available), and to execute them one by one at the same time as other jobs were being read in. The consequent additions to the rapidly growing operating system were a routine to handle the interrupts and a routine to decide which of the several jobs stored on disk was to be run next. This latter function, that of *scheduling*, derived from the introduction of disk (an essentially random access medium) as a replacement for magnetic tape (an essentially serial medium). A system working in this way was known as a *single-stream batch monitor* (single-stream meant that only one job was executed at a time); such systems were predominant in the mid 1960s.

The main disadvantage of a single-stream system was the dedication of the entire machine to the execution of a single job, no matter how large or small. This disadvantage was overcome by *multiprogramming* – the running of several programs in the same machine at the same time. The idea was that several programs (jobs) were held simultaneously in memory, and the central processor divided its time among them according to the resources (such as channels or peripherals) that each one needed at any instant. In this way it was theoretically possible, by having a suitable mix of jobs in the machine at any time, to achieve optimal utilisation of resources. This included central processor utilisation, as whenever a job was waiting for an I/O transfer to be completed the processor could switch to some other job currently in the machine. The additional load on the operating system was the control of resources and the protection of one job from the activities of another. An operating system of this type was called a *multi-stream batch monitor*, and versions abounded on all large computers of the early 1970s (for example, GEORGE 3 on the ICL 1900 series, and OS/360 on the IBM 360 and 370 series). The development of these systems owed much to the pioneering work done in the early 1960s on the Atlas computer at Manchester University.

At this stage of our historical progression from the raw machine we can see that there existed quite sophisticated systems which made good use of the hardware available. Their main disadvantage from the user's point of view was the lack of any interaction between user and job as it passed through the computer. Interaction is valuable in many situations, particularly during the development and debugging of a program; for example, debugging becomes easier if the programmer is immediately able to test modifications and see their effect, making further modifications as necessary. Similarly, many problem solving programs require 'steering' by the user; that is, the user directs the further action of the program after examining the results so far. In order for interaction to be feasible, the multi-stream batch system was modified to accept input from users typing at remote terminals; in other words, it became a multi-access system as described in the previous chapter. In the early 1970s most manufacturers produced multi-access operating systems for their larger computers; examples were MINIMOP (ICL 1900), TSS/360 (IBM 360 and 370), and TOPS-10 (DECSystem-10). By the mid 1970s the batch and multi-access modes of operation had been combined in such systems as MVS (IBM 370), VMS (DEC VAX), and System B (later known as VME) (ICL 2900 series).

Later developments in operating systems have concentrated on the provision of more sophisticated facilities designed to make better use of the hardware and software. Manufacturers have provided systems on which more than one operating system or machine instruction set may be run at the same time, thus providing a gradual upgrade path for customers; examples of this included VMS (DEC VAX) and CME (ICL 2900), both of which provided facilities for running programs developed on earlier ranges of hardware from the respective manufacturers. The VM system for the IBM 370 and descendants (Seawright *et al.*, 1979) allows the user to run any IBM operating system which can be run on the raw machine, but in parallel with other operating systems; apart from the increased functionality this also provides a useful testing environment. On the 80386 and 80486, OS/2 allows one to run multiple versions of MS-DOS and other operating systems designed for forerunners of those processors.

Another major development has been in *networking*; the evolution of better facilities for computer systems to communicate with each other. Batch systems are now less important than they used to be, and the emphasis has shifted from externally submitted jobs which generate printed output, to jobs submitted from interactive terminals which generate output into a file which may later be examined from a terminal. In fact, terminals have evolved from the simple teletype into sophisticated multi-windowed graphical devices such as the X terminal. Job control languages have also developed into more generalised facilities which can also be used at interactive terminals.

The foregoing discussion has led us to an operating system which must perform at least the following functions.

(1) Job sequencing

(2) Job control or command language interpretation

(3) Error handling

(4) I/O handling

(5) Interrupt handling

(6) Scheduling

(7) Resource control

(8) Protection

(9) Multi-access

Additionally, the operating system should be easy to run from the operator's point of view, and easy to control from the system manager's point of view. We can therefore add the further functions

(10) Provision of good interface to the operator

(11) Accounting of computing resource

It will be clear from this that operating systems are decidedly nontrivial animals, and it is not surprising that an enormous amount of effort has been spent in writing them. As a step towards a coherent structure for an operating system, we can abstract from the above list of functions certain characteristics which the system must exhibit. These, together with the attendant problems in displaying them, are listed in the following section.

2.2 Operating system characteristics

(1) Concurrency

Concurrency is the existence of several simultaneous, or parallel, activities. Examples are the overlapping of I/O operations with computation, and the coexistence in memory of several user programs. Concurrency raises problems of switching from one activity to another, of protecting one activity from the effects of another, and of synchronising activities which are mutually dependent.

(2) Sharing

Concurrent activities may be required to share resources or information. The motivation for this is fourfold.

(a) Cost: it is extravagant to provide sufficient resources for all users separately.

(b) Building on the work of others: it is useful to be able to use other people's programs or routines.

(c) Sharing data: it may be necessary to use the same data for several different programs, possibly working for several different users.

(d) Removing redundancy: it is economical to share a single copy of part or all of a program (for example an editor or a compiler) among several users, rather than provide a separate copy for each user or process.

Problems associated with sharing are resource allocation, simultaneous access to data, simultaneous execution of programs, and protection against corruption.

(3) Long-term storage

The need for sharing of programs and data implies the need for long-term storage of information. Long-term storage also allows users the convenience of keeping their programs or data in the computer rather than on some external medium. The problems arising are those of providing easy access, protection against interference (malicious or otherwise), and protection against system failure.

(4) Nondeterminacy

An operating system must be *determinate* in the sense that the same program, run today or tomorrow with the same data, should produce the same results. On the other hand it is *indeterminate* in that it must respond to events which will occur in an unpredictable order. These events are such things as resource requests, run-time errors in programs, and interrupts from peripheral devices. Because of the enormous number of contingencies that can arise, it is clearly unreasonable to expect to write the operating system to cater for them all individually. Instead, the system must be written so as to handle any sequence of events.

It is worth pointing out that none of these characteristics is peculiar to general purpose systems alone. Long-term storage, for example, is clearly required in file interrogation systems, and concurrency is a prime feature of transaction processing systems. Also, with the increasing power and complexity of personal computer systems, many of the above characteristics are important even on small single-user (but multiple process) systems.

To conclude this chapter we mention briefly a few features which it is desirable for a general purpose operating system to display.

2.3 Desirable features

(1) Efficiency

The need for efficiency has already been alluded to. Unfortunately, it is difficult to light on one single criterion by which the efficiency of an operating
system can be judged; various possible criteria are listed below.

(a) mean time between batch jobs (where applicable)

(b) unused central processor time (apart from time when the system has no
   work to do)

(c) turn-round time for batch jobs (where applicable)

(d) response time (in interactive systems)

(e) resource utilisation

(f) throughput (batch jobs per hour; rate at which work can be done
   interactively)

Not all these criteria can be satisfied simultaneously; we shall have more to
say in later chapters about design decisions which effectively give more weight
to some than to others. There is also the interesting question of whether human
resources are more expensive than machine resources; it may be better to
accept a less efficient aspect of a computer system if it provides a facility
which increases the overall efficiency of its users.

(2) Reliability

Ideally an operating system should be completely free of errors, and able to
handle all contingencies. In practice this is never the case, but we shall see in
chapter 10 how considerable progress can be made towards this goal.

(3) Maintainability

It should be possible to maintain an operating system – enhancing it or correcting errors – without employing an army of systems programmers. This implies
that the system should be modular in construction, with clearly defined interfaces between the modules, and that it should be well documented.

(4) Small size

Space used to hold the operating system, whether in memory or elsewhere, is
wasted so far as productive computing is concerned. Furthermore, a large
system is liable to be more prone to error, and will probably take longer to
develop, than a small one.

To summarise what has been covered in this chapter: we have discussed the general functions that we expect an operating system to fulfil; we have isolated some crucial operating system characteristics; and we have enumerated some desirable system features. In the next chapter we shall examine some basic tools which will help us to construct the system we require.

3   Concurrent Processes

Before we can start a detailed study of operating systems, we need to introduce some basic concepts and develop a few tools. This will be the purpose of the present chapter.

3.1 Programs, processes and processors

We start by considering an operating system as a set of activities, each providing one of the functions, such as scheduling or I/O, described in chapter 2. Each activity consists of the execution of one or more programs, and will be invoked whenever the corresponding function is to be provided. We use the word *process* to describe an activity of this kind. (Other names in the literature are *task* and *computation*.) A process may thus be thought of as a sequence of actions, performed by executing a sequence of instructions (a program), whose net result is the provision of some system function. We can extend this concept to include the provision of user functions as well as system functions, so that the execution of a user program is also called a process.

A process may involve the execution of more than one program; conversely, a single program or routine may be involved in more than one process. For example, a routine for adding an item to a list might be used by any process engaged in queue manipulation. Hence the knowledge that a particular program is currently being executed does not tell us much about what activity is being pursued or what function is being implemented. It is largely for this reason that the concept of a process is more useful than that of a program when talking about operating systems.

A process is able to proceed by virtue of an agent which executes the associated program. This agent is known as a *processor*. We say that a processor *runs* a process, or that a process *runs on* a processor. A processor is something which executes instructions; depending on the nature of the instructions the processor may be implemented in hardware alone, or in a combination of both hardware and software. For example, a central processing unit (CPU) is a processor for executing machine language instructions, while a CPU together with an interpreter for a particular programming language can form a processor for executing instructions expressed in that programming language. The transformation, discussed in chapter 1, of a raw computer into a virtual machine may in fact be regarded as the combination of the computer hardware and the operating system to provide a processor capable of running user processes (that is, a processor capable of executing user instructions).

The program or programs associated with a process need not be implemented as software. The action of a channel, for example, in performing a data transfer, may be looked on as a process in which the associated program is wired into the channel hardware. Viewed in this way the channel, or indeed any peripheral device, is a processor which is capable of executing only a single process.

The concepts of process and processor can readily be used to interpret both concurrency and nondeterminacy, which were two of the operating system characteristics outlined in the last chapter.

Concurrency can be regarded as the activation of several processes (that is, the execution of several programs) at the same time. Provided that there are as many processors as processes this presents no logical difficulty. If, as is more usual, there are fewer processors than processes then apparent concurrency can be obtained by switching processors from one process to another. If the switching is done at suitably small intervals of time then the system will give the illusion of concurrency when viewed on a longer time scale. Apparent concurrency is in effect achieved by interleaving processes on a single processor.

It may be helpful at this point to draw an analogy with the activities of a secretary in a general office. Each of the jobs a secretary has to perform, such as typing letters, filing invoices, or taking dictation, can be likened to a process in an operating system. The processor is the secretary, and the sequence of instructions which defines each job is analogous to a program. If the office is busy then the secretary may have to break off one job to do another, and in this situation the secretary would probably complain of 'doing several jobs at the same time'. Of course he or she is only doing one job at once, but the frequent switching from one activity to another gives an overall impression of concurrency. We may pursue the analogy further by observing that before the secretary can change to another activity a note must be made of what activity is currently being performed, in order to pick up the thread again later. Similarly, a processor in a computing system must record information about the process it is currently running before it can switch to some other process. The precise nature of the information to be stored will be discussed in the next chapter; for the moment we observe only that it must be sufficient to enable the process to be resumed at some later time.

Carrying the analogy still further, we can introduce additional secretaries (processors) into the office. True concurrency can now exist between the various secretaries performing different tasks, though apparent concurrency may still persist as each secretary switches from one task to another and back again. Only when the number of secretaries is equal to the number of jobs to be done can all the jobs be performed in a truly concurrent manner. The analogue of the processor, such as an I/O device, which can perform only a single process, is the junior secretary who is capable only of making the tea.

Bearing in mind the foregoing discussion, we define *concurrent processing* (or *parallel processing*) to mean that if a snapshot is taken of the system as a whole then several processes may be found somewhere between their starting points and their end points. This definition clearly includes both true and apparent concurrency.

Nondeterminacy is the second operating system characteristic which can easily be described in terms of processes. If we regard processes as sequences of actions which can be interrupted between steps, then nondeterminacy is reflected in the unpredictable order in which the interruptions may occur, and hence the unpredictable order in which the sequences proceed. Reverting to our secretarial analogy, we can liken the unpredictable events which occur in an operating system to telephones ringing in an office. It cannot be known in advance when a particular telephone will ring, how long it will take to deal with the call, or what effect the call will have on the various jobs being done in the office. We can observe, however, that the secretary who answers the telephone must make a note of the current task so that it can be returned to later. Similarly, the interruption of a process must be accompanied by the recording of information which will subsequently enable the process to be resumed. The information recorded is the same as that required when processors switch among processes in order to achieve concurrency. Indeed, interruption of a process can be regarded as a switch, caused by some unpredictable event, of a processor away from the process.

We can summarise what has been said so far as follows. A process is a sequence of actions, and is therefore dynamic, whereas a program is a sequence of instructions, and is therefore static. A processor is an agent for running a process. Nondeterminacy and concurrency can be described in terms of interrupting processes between actions and of switching processors among processes. In order to effect interruption and switching, sufficient information about a process must be stored in order that it may later be resumed.

3.2 Communication between processes

The processes within a computing system do not of course act in isolation. On the one hand they must co-operate to achieve the desired objective of running user jobs; on the other hand they are in competition for the use of limited resources such as processors, memory or files. The two elements of co-operation and competition imply the need for some form of communication between processes. The areas in which communication is essential may be categorised as follows.

(1) Mutual exclusion

System resources may be classed as *shareable*, meaning that they may be used by several processes concurrently (in the sense defined in the previous section), or *non-shareable*, meaning that their use is restricted to one process at a time. The non-shareability of a resource derives from one of two reasons.

(a) The physical nature of the resource makes it impracticable for it to be shared. A typical example is a printer, where it is impracticable to switch between the sheets of paper being printed for different processes.

(b) The resource is such that if it were used by several processes concurrently the actions of one process could interfere with those of another. A particularly common example is a memory location which contains a variable accessible to more than one process: if one process tests the variable while another modifies it then the result will be unpredictable and usually disastrous. For instance, suppose that in an airline booking system the availability of a particular seat is represented by the contents of a certain location in memory. Then if the location were accessible to more than one process at a time it would be possible for two travel agents to reserve the seat simultaneously by following the unfortunate sequence of actions below.

Agent A sees the seat is free
and consults his or her client

               .

               .   Agent B sees the seat is free

               .   and consults his or her client

               .   .

Agent A reserves   .
the seat   .

                                            .

                                          Agent B reserves
                                          the seat

Non-shareable resources therefore include most peripherals, writeable files, and data areas which are subject to modification; shareable resources include CPUs, read-only files, and areas of memory which contain pure procedures or data protected against modification. The mutual exclusion problem is that of ensuring that non-shareable resources are accessed by only one process at a time.

(2) Synchronisation

Generally speaking, the speed of one process relative to another is unpredictable, since it depends on the frequency of interruption of each process and on how often and for how long each process is granted a processor. We say that processes run *asynchronously* with respect to each other. However, to achieve successful co-operation there are certain points at which processes must synchronise their activities. These are points beyond which a process cannot proceed until another process has completed some activity. For example, a process which schedules user jobs cannot proceed until an input process has read at least one job into the machine. Similarly, a computational process producing output may not be able to proceed until its previous output has been printed. It is the operating system's responsibility to provide mechanisms by which synchronisation can be effected.

(3) Deadlock

When several processes compete for resources it is possible for a situation to arise in which no process can continue because the resources each one requires are held by another. This situation is called *deadlock*, or *deadly embrace*. It is analogous to the traffic jam which occurs when two opposing streams of traffic, in trying to turn across each other's path, become completely immobilised because each stream occupies the road space needed by the other. The avoidance of deadlock, or the limitation of its effects, is clearly one of the functions of the operating system.

3.3 Semaphores

The most important single contribution towards interprocess communication was the introduction (Dijkstra, 1965) of the concept of *semaphores* and the primitive operations *wait* and *signal* which act on them. (*Wait* and *signal* are often referred to by Dijkstra's original names P and V which are the initial letters of the corresponding Dutch words. We shall, however, adopt the more recent and descriptive terminology.)

A semaphore is a non-negative integer which, apart from initialisation of its value, can be acted upon only by the operations *wait* and *signal*. These operations act only on semaphores, and their effect is defined as follows.

signal(s)

The effect is to increase the value of the semaphore s by one, the increase being regarded as an indivisible operation. Indivisibility implies that *signal(s)* is not equivalent to the assignment statement '$s := s + 1$'. For suppose that two processes A and B both wish to perform the operation '*signal(s)*' when the value of *s* is, say, 3. Then the value of *s* when both operations are complete will be 5. Suppose on the other hand that in similar circumstances both processes wished to execute '*s : = s + 1*'. This statement would be implemented as three operations on most hardware; read *s*, add one, and store *s*; this would be true even if a single machine instruction was used to increment *s*. There would be no guarantee that A completed all three operations before B started them; if it did not, each process could then assign the value 4 to *s*, and one of the desired increments would be lost. For more details, see the discussion on the implementation of *wait* and *signal* in Section 4.6.

wait(s)

The effect is to decrease the value of the semaphore *s* by 1 as soon as the result would be non-negative. Again the operation is indivisible. The *wait* operation implies a potential delay, for when it acts on a semaphore whose value is 0, the process executing the operation can proceed only when some other process has increased the value of the semaphore to 1 by a *signal* operation. The indivisibility of the operation means that if several processes are delayed then only one of them can successfully complete the operation when the semaphore becomes positive. No assumption is made about which process this is. The effects of the *wait* and *signal* operations may be summarised as

wait(s)   : **when** s > 0 **do** decrement *s*

signal (s)   : increment *s*

where *s* is any semaphore.

It can be seen from these definitions that every *signal* operation on a semaphore increases its value by 1 and every successful (that is, completed) *wait* operation decreases its value by 1. Hence the value of a semaphore is related to the number of *wait* and *signal* operations on it by the relation

$$val(sem) = C(sem) + ns(sem) - nw(sem) \qquad (3.1)$$

where

val(sem)   is the value of semaphore *sem*

C(sem)   is its initial value

ns(sem)   is the number of *signal* operations on it

nw(sem)   is the number of successful *wait* operations on it

But, by definition

$$val(sem) >= 0$$

Hence we derive the important relation

$$nw(sem) <= ns(sem) + C(sem) \qquad (3.2)$$

in which equality holds if and only if $val(sem) = 0$.

The relation 3.2 is invariant under *wait* and *signal* operations; that is, it is true however many operations are performed.

The implementation of semaphores and of the *wait* and *signal* operations will be discussed in the next chapter. For the present we shall take it for granted that they can be implemented, and use them to solve the problems listed earlier.

(1) Mutual exclusion

Non-shareable resources, whether peripherals, files, or data in memory, can be protected from simultaneous access by several processes by preventing the processes from concurrently executing the pieces of program through which access is made. These pieces of program are called *critical sections*, and mutual exclusion in the use of resources can be regarded as mutual exclusion in the execution of critical sections. For example, processes may be mutually excluded from accessing a table of data if all the routines which read or update the table are written as critical sections such that only one may be executed at once.

Exclusion can be achieved by the simple expedient of enclosing each critical section by *wait* and *signal* operations on a single semaphore whose initial value is 1. Thus each critical section is programmed as

> *wait(mutex)*;
> > critical section
> *signal(mutex)*;

where *mutex* is the name of a semaphore. The reader will see by inspection that if the initial value of *mutex* is 1 then mutual exclusion is indeed assured, since at most one process can execute *wait(mutex)* before another executes *signal(mutex)*. More formally, application of relation 3.2 gives

$$nw(mutex) <= ns(mutex) + 1$$

which implies that at most one process can be inside its critical section at any time. Furthermore, a process is never unnecessarily prevented from entering its critical section; entry is prevented only if some other process is already inside its own critical section. We can see this by observing that a process is denied entry only if the value of *mutex* is 0. In this case relation 3.2 indicates that

$$nw(mutex) = ns(mutex) + 1$$

In other words the number of successful *wait* operations on *mutex* exceeds the number of *signal* operations by 1, which implies that some process is within its critical section.

Our conclusion is that each time a process wishes to access a shared variable or a shared resource then it must effect the access via a critical section which is protected by a semaphore as above.

As an example, suppose that an operating system contains two processes A and B which respectively add items to and remove items from a queue. In order that the queue pointers do not become confused it may be necessary to restrict access to the queue to only one process at a time. Thus the addition and removal of items would be coded as critical sections as below.

Program for Process A   *Program for Process B*

```
.
.
.
wait(mutex);              wait(mutex);
    add item to queue;        remove item from queue;
signal(mutex);            signal(mutex);
.                         .
.                         .
.                         .
```

At this point the suspicious reader may wonder whether the mutual exclusion problem could have been solved without the additional formalism of semaphores and their associated operations. On the face of it this suspicion might appear well founded, for it seems possible to derive a solution by protecting each critical section by a single simple variable (called *gate*, say). When *gate* is set to *open* (represented by the value 1, say), entry to the critical section is allowed; when it is set to closed (represented by 0), entry is not allowed. Thus a critical section would be coded as

while *gate = closed* **do** null operation;
gate := closed;
    critical section
gate =: open;

Thus each process entering the critical section tests that *gate* is *open* (and loops until it is); it then sets *gate* to *closed*, preventing other processes entering the section. On exit, the process resets *gate* to *open*, freeing the section for execution by another process.

Unfortunately this simple solution will not work. The reason lies in the separation of the test for an open *gate* in line 1 from the closing of *gate* in line 2. As a consequence of this separation two processes executing in parallel may each find an open *gate* at line 1 before either has the chance to close it at line 2. The result is that both processes enter the critical section together.

Semaphores avoid a similar difficulty by the insistence that the *wait* and *signal* operations are indivisible; there is no possibility of two processes acting on the same semaphore at the same time. The implementation of semaphores, to be discussed in chapter 4, must of course ensure that this is so.

(2) Synchronisation

The simplest form of synchronisation is that a process A should not proceed beyond a point L1 until some other process B has reached L2. Examples of this situation arise whenever A requires information at point L1 which is provided by B when it reaches L2. The synchronisation can be programmed as follows

   Program for Process A   *Program for Process B*

                    .   .
                    .   .
   L1: *wait(proceed)*;   L2: *signal(proceed)*;
                    .   .
                    .   .

where *proceed* is a semaphore with initial value 0.

It is clear from the above programs that A cannot proceed beyond L1 until B has executed the *signal* operation at L2. (Of course, if B executes the *signal* operation before A reaches L1 then A is not delayed at all.) Again we can use relation 3.2 to demonstrate this more formally; we have

$$nw(proceed) <= ns(proceed) \tag{3.3}$$

which implies that A cannot pass L1 before B passes L2.

The above example is asymmetric in that the progress of A is regulated by that of B but not vice versa. The case in which two processes each regulate the progress of the other is exemplified by the classic problem of the producer and consumer. Since this problem is typical of many which arise in interprocess communication we shall describe it in some detail.

A set of 'producer' processes and a set of 'consumer' processes communicate by means of a buffer into which the producers deposit items and from which the consumers extract them. The producers continually repeat the cycle 'produce item – deposit item in buffer', and the consumers repeat a similar cycle 'extract item from buffer – consume item'. A typical producer might be a computational process placing lines of output in a buffer, while the corresponding consumer might be the process which prints each line. The buffer is of limited capacity, being large enough to hold N items of equal size. The synchronisation required is twofold: firstly, the producers cannot put items into the buffer if it is already full, and secondly, the consumers cannot extract items if the buffer is empty. In other words, if the number of items deposited is d, and the number of items extracted is e, we must ensure that

$$0 <= d - e <= N$$

Furthermore, the buffer must be protected from simultaneous access by several processes, lest the actions of one (for example in updating pointers) disturb the actions of another. Hence both the deposition and extraction of items must be coded as critical sections.

We postulate the following solution to the problem

Program for producers	*Program for consumers*
repeat indefinitely	**repeat** indefinitely
begin	**begin**
produce item;	*wait(item available)*;
wait(space available);	*wait(buffer manipulation)*;
wait(buffer manipulation);	extract item from buffer;
deposit item in buffer;	*signal(buffer manipulation)*;
signal(buffer manipulation);	*signal(space available)*;
signal(item available);	consume item;
end;	**end;**

Synchronisation is achieved through the semaphores *space available* and *item available* whose initial values are N and 0 respectively. Mutual exclusion of processes from accessing the buffer is effected by the semaphore *buffer manipulation* with initial value 1.

We must now show that this solution satisfies relation 3.3. If we apply the invariance relation 3.2 to the two synchronisation semaphores we obtain

$$nw(space\ available) <= ns(space\ available) + N \qquad (3.4)$$

and

$$nw(item\ available) <= ns(item\ available) \qquad (3.5)$$

But we observe from the order of operations in the program for the producers that

$$ns(item\ available) <= d <= nw(space\ available) \qquad (3.6)$$

and from the order of operations in the program for the consumers that

$$ns(space\ available) <= e <= nw(item\ available) \qquad (3.7)$$

Hence, from relation 3.6

$$
\begin{aligned}
d \ &<= nw(space\ available) \\
&<= ns(space\ available) + N \qquad &\text{by 3.4} \\
&<= e + N \qquad &\text{by 3.7}
\end{aligned}
$$

Similarly, from relation 3.7

e $<=$ *nw*(*item available*)

$<=$ *ns*(*item available*)   by 3.5

$<= d$ by 3.6

Combination of these two results gives

$e <= d <= e + N$

which shows that relation 3.3 is satisfied as required.

The solution to the producer-consumer problem can be used as a guide in any situation where one process passes information to another. In particular, processes which drive input peripherals act as producers for those processes which consume the input, and processes which drive output peripherals act as consumers for those processes which produce the output.

(3) Deadlock

As pointed out earlier, deadlock can occur whenever a set of processes compete for resources. As such it is a problem that we will leave for full discussion until chapter 8.

In this section we remark that deadlock may also occur because processes are waiting for each other to complete certain actions. As an example, consider two processes A and B which operate on semaphores X and Y as below.

Process A	*Process B*
.	.
.	.
.	.
wait(X);	*wait*(Y);
.	.
.	.
wait(Y);	*wait*(X);
.	.
.	.

If the initial values of X and Y are 1 then each process can complete its first *wait* operation, reducing the semaphore values to 0. Clearly, neither process can then proceed beyond its next *wait* operation, and deadlock prevails.

The situation is in fact analogous to that in which deadlock arises from competing resource requests. If a semaphore is regarded as a resource, and *wait* and *signal* operations are regarded as claiming and releasing it, then deadlock has ensued because both A and B hold the resource required by the other. The 'shareability' of a semaphore is determined by its initial value: if the value is n (>1) the semaphore can be shared by n processes; if it is 1 (as above) then the semaphore is unshareable.

A similar but more complex case of deadlock can be derived from the producer-consumer problem by reversing the order of the *wait* operations performed by the consumers. If the buffer is empty it is possible for a consumer to gain access to the buffer by executing '*wait(buffer manipulation)*' and then to be suspended on '*wait(item available)*'. However, no producer can gain access to the buffer since it is held by the blocked consumer. Hence deadlock results. Again the situation is analogous to that resulting from competing resource requests. In this case the resources are the buffer, held by the consumer, and a new item, held by a producer.

The lesson to be learned from these examples is that deadlock can occur as a result of an incorrectly ordered sequence of *wait* operations even when no explicit resource requests are being made. It may be salutary to realise that the deadlock threat inherent in the wrong solution to the producer-consumer problem would not be detected by the validation carried out in the last section. Both the deadlock-free and deadlock-prone solutions satisfy relation 3.3, and thus appear equally correct by that criterion. Criteria for recognising deadlock in respect of resource allocation will be discussed in chapter 8; the recognition of deadlock (or lack of it) in a sequence of *wait* operations can be performed by an analysis similar to the following.

Consider the solution to the producer-consumer problem given in section (2) above. We shall show that it is in fact deadlock-free. Firstly we observe that the inner sections of the programs for the producers and consumers are simply critical sections protected by the semaphore *buffer manipulation*, and therefore in themselves possess no deadlock potential. Hence deadlock can prevail only if

   (a) no producer can pass *wait(space available)* and no consumer is in a
       position to execute *signal(space available)* (that is, no consumer is
       extracting);

and

   (b) no consumer can pass *wait(item available)* and no producer is in a
       position to execute *signal(item available)* (that is, no producer is
       depositing).

Condition (a), with relation 3.2, implies

   $nw(space\ available) = ns(space\ available) + N$

and

   $nw(item\ available) = ns(space\ available)$

Condition (b), with relation 3.2, implies

$nw(item\ available) = ns(item\ available)$

and

$nw(space\ available) = ns(item\ available)$

Putting these relations together we get

$nw(space\ available) = nw(space\ available) + N$

which is a contradiction (since $N > 0$).

A similar analysis for the case in which the order of *wait* operations in the consumer program is reversed is not possible, since the inner section of the program for the consumers is no longer a simple critical section (it now contains a *wait* operation). A more complex analysis (for example, Habermann, 1972; Lister, 1974) is needed to show that deadlock can in fact occur.

3.4 Monitors

In the previous section we saw how semaphores can be used to effect synchronisation and communication between processes. The undisciplined use of semaphores is, however, rather prone to error – a programmer can easily place *wait* and *signal* operations in the wrong places, or even omit them altogether. For example, a programmer who fails to realise that a particular data structure is to be shared by several processes will omit to enclose in *wait* and *signal* operations the critical sections of program which access it. The data structure will then be unprotected from simultaneous manipulation by several processes, and inconsistencies in its contents will probably ensue.

To avoid such problems there have been a number of proposals for programming language constructs which oblige the programmer to declare shared data and resources explicitly, and which enforce mutual exclusion of access to such shared objects. One of the most influential and widely adopted constructs is the *monitor* (Hoare, 1974), which we describe briefly below, and in more detail in the Appendix.

A monitor consists of

(1) the data comprising a shared object

(2) a set of procedures which can be called to access the object

(3) a piece of program which initialises the object (this program is executed only once, when the object is created)

For example, a buffer (such as that described in the previous section) for passing data items between producer processes and consumer processes might be represented by a monitor consisting of

(1) the buffer space and pointers (for example, an array, and indices into it)

(2) two procedures *deposit* and *extract* which can be called by processes to place an item in the buffer or remove an item from it

(3) a piece of program which initialises the buffer pointers to the start of the buffer

The compiler for a language incorporating monitors must ensure that access to a shared object can be made only by calling a procedure of the corresponding monitor (this can be achieved fairly easily through the scope mechanism of most block structured languages). The compiler must also ensure that the procedures of each monitor are implemented as mutually exclusive critical sections. The compiler may well do this by generating *wait* and *signal* operations on appropriate semaphores in the compiled program. Thus, in the buffer example, the compiler guarantees that access to the buffer is restricted to the *deposit* and *extract* procedures, and that these procedures are mutually exclusive.

It should be apparent that monitors eliminate a potentially fertile source of errors by transferring the responsibility for mutual exclusion from the programmer to the compiler. Responsibility for other forms of synchronisation remains, however, with the programmer, who must use semaphores (or something equivalent) to effect it. For example, the representation of a buffer as a monitor (as above) ensures through the mutual exclusion of *deposit* and *extract* that items cannot be simultaneously inserted and removed. It does not, however, prevent processes depositing items in a full buffer or removing them from an empty one. Such disasters must be prevented by placing appropriate synchronisation operations inside the *deposit* and *extract* procedures. The details are given in the Appendix.

The monitor construct has been implemented in a number of programming languages, such as Concurrent Pascal (Hansen, 1975), Pascal-plus (Welsh and Bustard, 1979), Mesa (Lampson and Redell, 1980), and Turing (Holt and Cordy, 1988). For the operating system implementor it has the advantage of restricting all operations on a shared object to a set of well defined procedures, and of ensuring that these operations are mutually exclusive. Synchronisation for purposes other than mutual exclusion remains the responsibility of the programmer.

3.5 Message passing

Some systems (in particular, client-server systems – recall section 1.2) implement interprocess communication and synchronisation by passing *messages* between processes. Message passing is especially interesting, because there is no reason why the communicating processes should be required to run on the same processor or computer, provided, of course, that there is a hardware communication link between them.

The primitives provided by the operating system allow processes to *send* and receive *messages*. For example, the procedures provided could be

> send_message(*destination*, *message*);

and

> receive_message(*source*, *message*);

where

> *destination* identifies the process which is to receive the message
>
> *source* identifies the process from which a message is required
>
> *message* is a reference to a memory area containing the message

Each of the above primitives generally takes two forms: *blocking* and *non-blocking*. A blocking send operation waits until the receiving process accepts the message; a nonblocking send simply places the message in some form of queue and allows the sender to continue execution. A blocking receive operation waits for a message to be sent to the process (unless there is one already waiting to be accepted); a nonblocking receive accepts a message if one is waiting, otherwise it returns some indication that no message was available. Nonblocking message handling requires that the operating system provide some kind of buffer area, or *message pool*, into which waiting messages can be copied and held while awaiting acceptance; this increases the availability of the sending process, at the expense of some system memory.

The identification of processes also has variants. The destination process may be specified with an especial identifier which indicates that the message is to be sent to a group of processes, or even all processes; this is a *broadcast* message. In a similar way, the source process may be specified as any one of a group of processes, or as any process in the system; this might be used where a server process is prepared to accept work from any other process in the system.

We have not yet said what constitutes a message. Typically, messages are short (a few bytes or tens of bytes); it is easier if they are of a fixed size, since this simplifies the management of any buffer space. Messages from client processes to server processes usually contain an indication of the service requested, together with any necessary parameters. Any further information needed by the server is generally imparted by passing a reference to an area in shared memory where such information is to be found.

Message passing has been used in many systems; for example, MU5 (Morris and Ibbett, 1979), Thoth (Cheriton, 1979), MINIX (Tanenbaum, 1987) and OS/2 (Deitel and Kogan, 1992).

3.6 Summary

In this chapter we have introduced the notion of a process, as opposed to a program, and have shown that it is a useful concept in the study of operating system characteristics. In particular we have seen that both concurrency and nondeterminacy can be described in terms of switching processors between processes. We have also introduced semaphores and the operations on them as one mechanism for interprocess communication, and have demonstrated that they are a sufficient tool for solving problems of mutual exclusion and synchronisation.

We briefly mentioned monitors and message passing as alternative mechanisms for interprocess communication, but for the sake of specificity we will confine ourselves to semaphores as we build the paper operating system in the rest of this book.

4 The System Nucleus

In the last chapter we developed the concepts and tools needed to build the paper operating system outlined in chapter 1. As mentioned there, the paper operating system will resemble an onion in which each layer provides a set of functions dependent only on the layers within it. At the centre of the onion are the facilities provided by the hardware of the machine itself. The onion layers can be regarded as implementing successive virtual machines, so that the onion as a whole implements the virtual machine required by the user.

The major interface between the basic machine hardware and the operating system is provided by the system *nucleus*, which is the innermost layer of the onion. The purpose of the nucleus is to provide an environment in which processes can exist; this implies handling interrupts, switching processors between processes, and implementing mechanisms for interprocess communication. Before describing these functions in detail we shall look at the essential hardware required to support the operating system that we are trying to build.

4.1 Essential hardware facilities

(1) Interrupt mechanism

It was mentioned in chapter 2 that in order for I/O activities to be overlapped with central processing it must be possible to interrupt the running process when a peripheral transfer is complete. We therefore demand that our computer should provide an interrupt mechanism which at least saves the value of the program counter for the interrupted process and transfers control to a fixed location in memory. This location will be used as the start of a piece of program known as an *interrupt routine*, *interrupt service routine*, or *interrupt handler*, whose purpose is to determine the source of the interrupt and to respond to it in an appropriate manner. We will describe the interrupt handler in section 4.4, and will discuss the various forms it can take according to the precise nature of the interrupt mechanism available.

(For the sake of completeness we mention that some computers, for example the CDC CYBER 170 range, operated without an explicit interrupt mechanism. In such a computer one or more processors had to be dedicated to monitoring the state of the I/O devices to detect when transfers were complete.

In the case of the CYBER this function was performed by a number of so-called 'peripheral processors', while the CPU was relieved of all I/O handling. A restricted form of interrupt still existed, however, since the peripheral processors could force the CPU to jump to a different location.)

(2) Memory protection

When several processes are running concurrently, it is necessary to protect the memory used by one process from unauthorised access by another. The protection mechanisms which must be built into the memory addressing hardware are described in detail in the next chapter; for the present we take their existence for granted.

(3) Privileged instruction set

In order that concurrent processes cannot interfere with each other, part of the instruction set of the computer must be reserved for use by the operating system only. These privileged instructions perform such functions as

- (a) enabling and disabling interrupts
- (b) switching a processor between processes
- (c) accessing registers used by the memory protection hardware
- (d) performing input or output
- (e) halting a central processor, and controlling its operation (for example, enabling and disabling internal mechanisms such as floating point accelerator units and memory caches)

To distinguish between times when privileged instructions are allowed and times when they are not, most computers operate in more than one mode. Typically there are two modes, often known as *supervisor mode* and *user mode*. Privileged instructions can be used only in supervisor mode. The switch from user to supervisor mode is made automatically in any of the following circumstances.

- (a) A user process calls on the operating system to execute some function requiring the use of a privileged instruction. Such a call is termed a *supervisor call* or *system call*; another, older, term is *extracode*.
- (b) An interrupt occurs.
- (c) An error condition occurs in a user process. The condition can be treated as an 'internal interrupt', and is handled in the first instance by an interrupt routine.
- (d) An attempt is made to execute a privileged instruction while in user mode. The attempt can be regarded as a particular kind of error, and is handled as in (c) above.

The switch from supervisor mode back to user mode is effected by an instruction which is itself privileged.

As mentioned above, there may be more than two levels of privilege. For example, the Intel 80486 and the DEC VAX have four levels, and the ICL 2900 has as many as 16. We shall defer discussion of such multilevel machines until chapter 9.

(4) Real-time clock

A hardware clock, which interrupts at fixed intervals of real-time (that is, time as measured in the outside world rather than time required for computation by any particular process), is essential for the implementation of scheduling policies and for the accounting of resources consumed by the various users.

We shall assume from this point that the machine on which we are building our paper operating system has the hardware facilities outlined above. More precisely, since we allow the possibility of including several central processors in a single configuration, we shall assume that each processor has facilities (1) to (3) and that there is a single real-time clock which can interrupt each processor. In addition we shall restrict ourselves to *tightly coupled* configurations; that is, those in which the processors are identical and share a common memory. This excludes consideration of computer networks, in which the processors have separate memories and communicate by some form of data transmission. It also excludes systems in which dissimilar processors are organised so as to share a workload in a way best suited to their particular characteristics. The former topic merits a book on its own; the latter is still a fertile field in which no clear trends have yet emerged.

4.2 Outline of the nucleus

The relationship between the nucleus and the rest of the operating system is illustrated in figure 4.1. The horizontal line at the base of the diagram represents the computer hardware; the thickened portion of this line is the privileged instruction set, whose use we restrict to the nucleus. (Exceptions to this rule are some privileged instructions concerned with memory protection and I/O; these are discussed in later chapters.) The nucleus consists of three pieces of program

(1) the first level interrupt handler, which performs the initial handling of all interrupts;

(2) the dispatcher, which switches the central processors between processes;

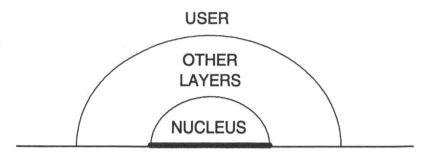

Figure 4.1 Structure of the paper operating system

(3) two procedures (routines) which implement the interprocess communication primitives (for example, *wait* and *signal*) described in chapter 3. These procedures are called via system calls in the processes concerned.

Because the nucleus is built directly on the basic hardware, we can expect it to be the most heavily machine dependent part of an operating system. Indeed it is probably the only part of an operating system likely to be written substantially in assembly language. With a few small exceptions, mainly related to I/O, the other layers can be most conveniently (and reliably) written in a high level language. Suitable systems programming languages, to which the reader may care to refer, are BCPL (Richards, 1979), BLISS (Wulf *et al.*, 1971), C (Kernighan and Ritchie, 1978), and C++ (Ellis and Stroustrup, 1990). Other languages, like Concurrent Pascal (Hansen, 1975) and Modula (Wirth, 1977 and 1983), are intended specifically for writing operating systems, though they impose certain constraints on the system designer.

The restriction of assembly language to one small part (probably no more than 400 instructions) of the operating system, made possible by the system's hierarchical structure, can contribute greatly towards realising the goal of an error free, comprehensible, and maintainable product. It is worth noting that some systems programming languages sometimes allow the inclusion of embedded machine instructions within the high level language constructs; this often means that a module which would otherwise need to be written in assembly language can be coded almost completely in the high level language, with the presence of the occasional machine instruction only where it is needed to define an operation which cannot be expressed directly in the main language.

4.3 Representation of processes

The programs within the nucleus are responsible for maintaining the environment in which processes exist. Consequently they are required to operate on some data structure which is the physical representation of all processes within the system. The nature of this data structure is the concern of the current section.

Each process can be represented by a *process descriptor* (sometimes known as a *process control block* or *state vector*) which is an area of memory containing all relevant information about the process. The composition of this information will become apparent as we progress; for the present we include in it some identification of the process (the *process name*) and an indication of the *status* of the process. A process can have one of three main values for its status: it may be *running*, which means that it is currently executing on a processor; it may be *runnable*, meaning that it could run if a processor were allocated to it; or it may be *unrunnable*, meaning that it could not use a processor even if one were allocated. The most common reason for a process being unrunnable is that it is waiting for the completion of a peripheral transfer. The status of a process is an essential piece of information for the dispatcher when it comes to allocate a central processor.

A process which is running on a central processor is known as the *current process* for that processor; the number of current processes within the system at any time is of course less than or equal to the number of processors available.

A further part of the process descriptor can be used to store all information about the process which needs to be saved when it loses control of a processor. This information, required for subsequent resumption of the process, includes the values of all machine registers, such as program counter, general purpose registers, and index registers, which could be changed by another process. It also includes the values of any registers used in addressing the memory used by the process (see chapter 5). The format of this part of the process descriptor is often dictated by hardware, because the privileged instruction which switches the central processor into user mode has to 'know' where to find the new contents of the various registers, and any entry to supervisor mode has to save these registers back into the same places. This part of the process descriptor is sometimes known separately as the *hardware process descriptor*. All of the information saved and restored here is called the *volatile environment* of the process (other names in the literature are *process context* and *process state*). More formally, the volatile environment of a process can be defined as that subset of the modifiable shared facilities of the system which are accessible to the process.

The process descriptor of each process is linked into a *process structure*, which acts as a description of all processes within the system. For the present we shall adopt an elementary form of process structure, in which the process descriptors are linked into a simple list. The process structure is the first data structure we have introduced into our operating system; since it will be by no means the last, we also introduce a *central table* whose purpose is to serve as a

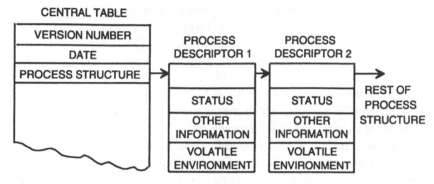

Figure 4.2 Central table and process structure

means of access to all system structures. The central table will contain a pointer to each data structure, and may also be used to hold any other global information, such as the date, time of day, and system version number, which might from time to time be required. The central table and process structure are illustrated in figure 4.2.

4.4 The first level interrupt handler

The first level interrupt handler (FLIH) is the part of the operating system which is responsible for responding to signals both from the outside world (interrupts) and from within the computing system itself (error traps and system calls). We shall refer collectively to both types of signal as interrupts and use the adjectives 'external' and 'internal' to distinguish between them where necessary. The function of the FLIH is twofold

(1) to determine the source of the interrupt

(2) to initiate service of the interrupt

The FLIH is always entered in supervisor mode, so that it has full access to the privileged instruction set; this is needed for obvious reasons.

We have already stated in section 4.1 that the computer's interrupt mechanism is responsible for saving at least the value of the program counter for the interrupted process. It must also be ensured that other registers required by the FLIH which may be being used by the interrupted process are appropriately saved. If this is not done by the interrupt mechanism, it must be performed as the first operation of the FLIH itself. Because the FLIH is a relatively simple program operating in a dedicated area of memory the set of registers involved will not be large, perhaps just a single general purpose register. It will certainly be considerably smaller than the volatile environment of the interrupted process, which need not be saved in its entirety since the same process may be resumed once the interrupt has been serviced.

An alternative strategy to saving register values, adopted for example on some of the PDP-11 range, and on the Am29000, is to provide a different set of registers. Sometimes the switch to the alternate set is achieved simply by changing modes (as in the PDP-11), and sometimes it is done by more complex means such as indirect register access (as on the Am29000). The FLIH can use these registers and leave those of the interrupted process intact.

Determination of the source of the interrupt can be performed more or less easily depending on the hardware provided. In the case of the most primitive hardware, in which all interrupts transfer control to the same location, identification must be achieved by a sequence of tests on the hardware status flags of all possible interrupt sources. This sequence, called a *skip chain*, is illustrated in figure 4.3. It is clearly advantageous to code the skip chain so that the most frequent sources of interrupts occur near its head.

On some computers (for example, the VAX and the 80486) the skip chain is rendered unnecessary by the inclusion of hardware which distinguishes between interrupt sources by transferring control to a different location for each source. This reduces the time to identify an interrupt at the cost of the extra interrupt locations required. A compromise arrangement employed on several computers, including the ICL 2900, and the IBM 370 series, is to provide a small number of interrupt locations each of which is shared by a group of devices. The first stage of interrupt identification is then achieved by hardware, and a short skip chain starting at each location is sufficient to complete it. The distinction between external interrupts, error traps, and system calls is often made in this way. The interrupt mechanism may give further aids to identification by placing information about the interrupt in a privileged register (as in the ICL 2900) or in some fixed memory location (as in the IBM 370).

Interrupts to a central processor are normally inhibited by hardware when control is transferred to the FLIH. This ensures that values of registers saved on entry to the FLIH cannot be overwritten by a subsequent interrupt occurring before the FLIH is left. Any interrupt which occurs while the interrupt mechanism is disabled is held pending until the mechanism is re-enabled on exit from the FLIH. This arrangement becomes inoperable in situations where some peripheral devices require response far more quickly than others if, for example, data is not to be lost. In these cases it is convenient to introduce the

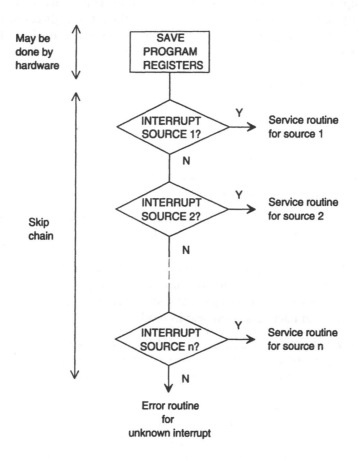

Figure 4.3 Interrupt identification by a skip chain

notion of *priority* among the interrupt sources, and to allow an interrupt routine itself to be interrupted by a request for service from a source of higher priority. Some computers (for example the IBM 370) allow this to be done by select- ively disabling interrupts within the FLIH; when the FLIH is servicing an interrupt it disables all those of equal or lower priority. Care must of course be taken to store the program registers of the interrupted process in different locations according to the priority level of the interrupt received. Alternatively, the interrupt hardware may itself distinguish between various priority levels, transferring control to and saving registers at different locations for each level. An interrupt at one level automatically inhibits others at the same or lower levels. The PDP-11, Motorola M68000 and DEC VAX are examples of pro- cessors with this kind of priority interrupt mechanism, the PDP-11 and M68000 each having eight levels while the VAX has 32.

The second function of the FLIH is to initiate service of an interrupt by calling an interrupt service routine appropriate to the type of interrupt involved. We shall give details in chapter 6 of service routines for I/O devices, and in chapter 11 of handling error traps. At this stage, we can say that because the interrupt routines effectively run in supervisor mode with interrupts wholly or partially disabled it is desirable to keep them as short as possible. In general each routine will perform some minimal action, for example transferring a character from an input device into a buffer, and then hand over responsibility for further action, such as reacting to the character received, to a process which runs in normal user mode. Sometimes this process will be the actual user process, but it may instead be a special purpose system process (often known as an Ancillary Control Process, or ACP) charged with the task of further processing of the data before handing it on to a user process. An ACP might be used for supporting a network, where it could take care of issues such as the handling of network protocols.

It is important to note that the occurrence of an interrupt, either external or internal, will often alter the status of some process. For instance, a process which has requested a peripheral transfer and which is unrunnable while the transfer is in progress will be made runnable again by the interrupt which occurs at its completion. Again, certain system calls, such as a *wait* operation on a zero valued semaphore or a request for I/O, will result in the current process being unable to continue. In all cases the change of status is effected by the interrupt routine changing the status entry in the process descriptor of the process concerned.

A consequence of the status change is that the process which was running on the processor concerned before the interrupt occurred may not be the most suitable to run afterwards. It may be the case, for example, that the interrupt makes runnable a process which in some sense has a higher priority than the currently running one. The question of when to switch a central processor between processes, and which process to favour, is considered in the next section.

4.5 The dispatcher

It is the function of the dispatcher (sometimes known as the *low-level scheduler*) to allocate the central processors among the various processes in the system. The dispatcher is entered whenever a current process cannot continue, or whenever there are grounds to suppose that a processor might be better employed elsewhere. These occasions may be detailed as follows

(1) after an external interrupt which changes the status of some process;

(2) after a system call which results in the current process being
temporarily unable to continue;

(3) after an error trap which causes suspension of the current process while
the error is dealt with.

These occasions are all special cases of interrupts; that is, they are all interrupts which alter the status of some process. For the sake of simplicity we do
not distinguish them from those interrupts, such as a *wait* operation on a positive valued semaphore, which have no effect on the status of any process; we
say, in effect, that the dispatcher is ultimately entered after *all* interrupts. The
overhead in entering the dispatcher on occasions when no process status has
changed is more than offset by the advantages gained by a uniform treatment
of all interrupts.

The operation of the dispatcher is quite simple, and is as follows.

(1) Is the current process on this processor still the most suitable to run? If
so, then return control to it at the point indicated by the program
counter stored by the interrupt hardware. If not, then...

(2) Save the volatile environment of the current process in its process
descriptor. Some machines (for example, the VAX) provide a single
machine instruction to do this.

(3) Retrieve the volatile environment of the most suitable process from its
process descriptor (again, this may be possible with a single machine
instruction).

(4) Transfer control to the newly selected process, at the location indicated
by the restored program counter.

When determining the most suitable process to run, it is sufficient to order all
runnable processes by some priority. The assignment of priorities to processes
is not the function of the dispatcher but of the high level scheduler to be
described in chapter 8. For the present we remark that priorities are calculated
according to such factors as the amount of resources required, the length of
time since the process last ran, and the relative 'importance' of the originating
user. As far as the dispatcher is concerned the process priorities are given *a
priori*.

In our paper operating system we link the process descriptors of all runnable processes into a queue ordered by decreasing priority, so that the most
eligible process is at its head. We call this queue the *processor queue*, illustrated in figure 4.4. Thus the role of the dispatcher is to run the first process on
the processor queue which is not already running on some other processor.
This may or may not be the same process which was running before the dispatcher was invoked.

We note in passing that the introduction of the processor queue means that the action taken by an interrupt routine to make a process runnable is now twofold. Firstly it must alter the status entry in the process descriptor and secondly it must link the process descriptor into the processor queue at the position indicated by its priority. We shall see in the next section that this operation can conveniently be done by executing a *signal* operation on a semaphore on which the process concerned has executed *wait*.

It is of course possible that at a particular moment the processor queue contains fewer processes than there are processors, perhaps because there are several processes waiting for input or output. This situation, which is probably the result of a poor high level scheduling decision, implies that there is no work for some central processors to do. Rather than allowing a processor to loop within the dispatcher it is convenient to introduce an extra process, called the *null process*, which has the lowest priority and is always runnable. The null process may be nothing more than an idle loop, or it may perform some useful

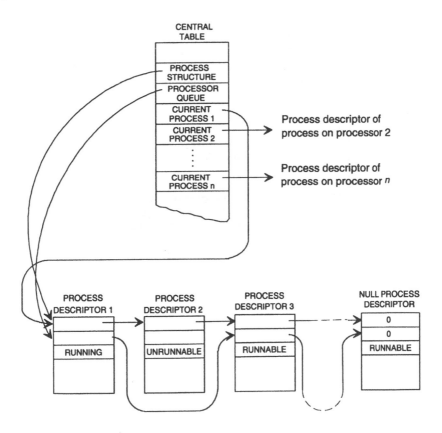

Figure 4.4 Process structure and processor queue

function such as executing processor test programs. Some machines (for example the PDP-11 and the ICL 2900) provide a special instruction for execution by the null process; this instruction suspends all machine operation until an interrupt occurs, and can reduce demands on the memory system which might slow down I/O. It has also been known for the null process to be used for such esoteric purposes as solving chess endgame problems or calculating the decimal expansion of π. Its position at the end of the processor queue is shown in figure 4.4.

The operation of the dispatcher can now be summarised as follows.

(1) Is the current process on this processor still the first non-running process on the processor queue? If so then resume it. If not, then...

(2) Save the volatile environment of the current process.

(3) Restore the volatile environment of the first non-running process in the processor queue.

(4) Resume running this process.

Before leaving the dispatcher we should point out that we have chosen a very simple structure for the runnable processes. Many operating systems divide the runnable processes into several classes, distinguished by such criteria as resources required, the maximum waiting time to be tolerated, or the amount

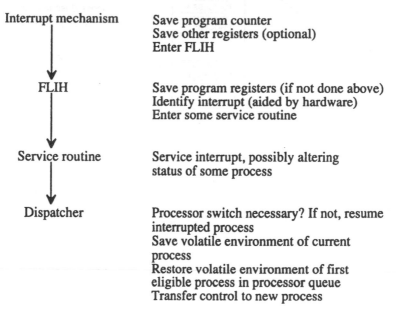

Figure 4.5 Relationship between the FLIH and the dispatcher

of processor time to be allowed before the process is pre-empted (the *quantum*).

One common variation is the *multilevel feedback queue*, first used on the CTSS system (Corbató, 1962). This system uses more than one processor queue; each queue has a particular quantum associated with it, this being smallest for the highest priority queue and largest for the lowest priority queue. Each queue is serviced on a first come, first served basis. A process is originally placed in the queue with the highest priority; if it runs for the whole of its allotted quantum it is relegated to the next queue down in priority (with a larger quantum); if it runs for the whole of its increased quantum it is relegated to the next queue down, and so on. The effect is to ensure that processes associated with on-line terminals, which typically have low processor requirements, receive a rapid service, whereas processor bound jobs receive longer but less frequent attention.

Another approach, used in VMS, is *priority boosting*. The initial priority (or *base priority*) assigned to a process is treated merely as a starting point; any process that takes certain defined actions (for example performing some kind of interaction with a terminal) is temporarily given a higher priority. Each time the process is subsequently chosen by the dispatcher its actual priority is reduced a little until it finally regains its base priority. This approach tends to give good interactive response at the expense of processes that perform little or no interaction.

We shall say more about this area when we discuss scheduling in chapter 8.

We conclude this chapter by summarising the relationship between the FLIH and the dispatcher in Figure 4.5.

4.6 Implementation of *wait* and *signal*

The final part of the nucleus is the implementation of some form of interprocess communication mechanism. As indicated in chapter 3 we shall use the operations *wait* and *signal* as our communication primitives, a choice which is based on the widespread understanding and ease of implementation of semaphores. Other communication mechanisms can be found in the literature (Andrews and Schneider, 1983). Some of these, like monitors (see section 3.4), may themselves be implemented in terms of semaphores.

Wait and *signal* are included in the nucleus because

(1) they must be available to all processes, and hence must be implemented at a low level;

(2) the *wait* operation may result in a process being blocked, causing an entry to the dispatcher to reallocate the process. Hence the *wait* operation must have access to the dispatcher;

(3) a convenient way for an interrupt routine to awaken (make runnable) a process is to execute *signal* on a semaphore on which the process has executed *wait*. Hence *signal* must be accessible to the interrupt routines.

The operations we have to implement (see chapter 3) are

wait(s)   : **when** $s > 0$ **do** decrement s

signal(s) : increment s

where s is any semaphore. We develop our implementation as follows.

(1) Blocking and unblocking

The *wait* operation implies that processes are blocked when a semaphore has value 0 and freed when a *signal* operation increases the value to 1. The natural way to implement this is to associate with each semaphore a semaphore queue. When a process performs an 'unsuccessful' *wait* operation (that is, it operates on a zero valued semaphore) it is added to the semaphore queue and made unrunnable. Conversely, when a *signal* operation is performed on a semaphore some process can be taken off the semaphore queue (unless empty) and be made runnable again. The semaphore must therefore be implemented with two components: an integer and a queue pointer (which may be null).

At this point our implementation is as follows

wait(s) :   **if** $s <> 0$ **then** $s := s - 1$
               else add process to semaphore queue and make unrunnable;

signal(s) : **if** queue empty **then** $s := s + 1$
               else remove some process from semaphore queue and make runnable;

Note that the semaphore need not be incremented within *signal* if a process is to be freed, since the freed process would immediately have to decrement the semaphore again in completing its *wait* operation.

(2) Queueing and dequeueing

We have said nothing yet about which process is lucky enough to be removed from the semaphore queue after a *signal* operation. Nor have we stated whether a process which is added to the queue on an unsuccessful *wait* operation should be added at the head, tail, or somewhere in the middle. In other words we have not yet specified the queue organisation.

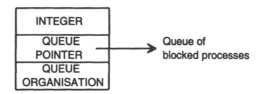

Figure 4.6 Structure of a semaphore

For most semaphores a simple first in, first out queue is adequate, since it ensures that all blocked processes are eventually freed. In some cases it may be preferable to order the queue on some other basis, perhaps by a priority similar to that used in the processor queue. This latter organisation ensures that processes with high processor priority do not languish for long periods of time on a semaphore queue. The important point is that different semaphores may require different queue organisations, so that an extra component must be included in the semaphore implementation to indicate which queue organisation applies. This component may simply be a coded description of the queue organisation, or in more complex cases it may be a pointer to a small piece of program which will perform the queueing and dequeueing operations. The structure of a semaphore in our implementation is shown in figure 4.6.

(3) Processor allocation

Both *wait* and *signal* may alter the status of a process, the former by making it unrunnable and the latter by doing the opposite. An exit must therefore be made to the dispatcher for a decision on which process to run next. In cases where no process status has changed (that is, a *wait* on a positive valued semaphore or a *signal* on a semaphore with an empty queue) the dispatcher will resume the current process since it will still be the first non-running process in the processor queue. It is arguable that in this case the return from *wait* or *signal* should be directly to the current process rather than via the dispatcher; the resulting gain in efficiency would be at the expense of a slight extra complexity in the code for *wait* and *signal*. In this discussion we shall opt for simplicity over efficiency, while recognising that the opposite viewpoint may be equally valid.

(4) Indivisibility

As pointed out in chapter 3, both *wait* and *signal* must be indivisible operations in the sense that only one process can be allowed to execute them at any time. Hence they must both be implemented as procedures which begin with some kind of *lock* operation and end with an *unlock* operation. On a single processor configuration the *lock* operation can most easily be implemented by disabling the interrupt mechanism. This ensures that a process cannot lose control of the central processor while executing *wait* and *signal* since there is no way in which it can be interrupted. The *unlock* operation is performed by simply re-enabling the interrupts. On a machine with several central processors this procedure is inadequate since it is possible for two processes simultaneously to enter *wait* or *signal* by running on separate processors. In this case we need some other mechanism, such as a 'test and set' instruction. This is an instruction which tests and modifies the content of a memory location in a single operation. During execution of the instruction, attempts by other processors to access the location are inhibited.

The idea is that a particular location is used as a flag (similar to the variable *gate* in section 3.3) which indicates whether entry to the *wait* and *signal* procedures is allowed. If the flag is not zero (say) entry is permitted, otherwise it is not. The *lock* operation consists of executing a test and set instruction on the flag, which determines its value and at the same time sets it to zero. If the value of the flag is not zero then the process proceeds, otherwise it loops on the test and set instruction until the process currently inside the *wait* or *signal* procedure unlocks the flag by setting it to some not zero value. Note that difficulties similar to those which arose in respect of the variable *gate* in section 3.3 are avoided by implementing the entire test and set instruction as a single indivisible operation. This lock and unlock mechanism is adopted on many computers, including the IBM 370 series and the DEC VAX.

An alternative to test and set, adopted on the Intel 80486 among others, is an instruction to interchange the contents of two memory locations. The lock operation starts by interchanging the values of a flag and a location which has previously been set to zero. The value of this second location is then examined to see whether entry is permitted, while any other process trying to gain entry will find the zero left by the interchange. A process which finds after the interchange that the flag was zero simply repeats the lock operation until the flag is made non-zero by some other process executing an unlock operation.

It should be noted that both these mechanisms imply some form of *busy waiting*. That is, a process which cannot pass the *lock* operation ties up its processor in a tight loop repeatedly trying the operation until the flag becomes unset. So long as the *wait* and *signal* procedures are simple the length of time involved in busy waiting should be quite short.

It is worth emphasising that the *lock* and *unlock* operations cannot be used as a substitute for *wait* and *signal*. The busy waiting or interrupt inhibition used to implement the *lock* operation would not be acceptable over the time scale for which processes can be delayed by a *wait* operation. The table below

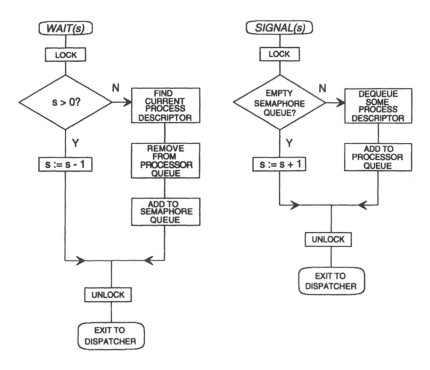

Figure 4.7 Implementation of wait and signal

shows the conceptually different levels at which the two kinds of operation exist.

The result of the foregoing discussion is that we can implement *wait* and *signal* as two related procedures as shown in figure 4.7. The procedures will be called by system calls which are part of the instruction repertoire of all processes.

	Wait and *Signal*	*Lock* and *Unlock*
Purpose	General process synchronisation	Mutual exclusion of processes from *wait* and *signal* procedures
Implementation level	Software	Hardware
Delaying mechanism	Queueing	Busy waiting/interrupt inhibition
Typical delay time	Several seconds	Several microseconds

We have now completed the system nucleus, which consists of the first level interrupt handler, the dispatcher and the procedures for *wait* and *signal*, all running in supervisor mode.

5 Memory Management

Memory management is the next layer of our 'onion'. We put it next to the nucleus because unless a process possesses some memory there is very little it can do. It certainly cannot execute, since there is no room for the associated program, nor can it perform input or output without space for buffers.

In this chapter we shall first of all discuss the objectives of memory management and introduce the concept of virtual memory. We shall then describe ways in which virtual memory can be implemented, and discuss various policies for regulating the implementation. Finally, we shall see how memory management can be included in our paper operating system.

5.1 Objectives

The objectives of memory management are fivefold.

(1) Relocation

In a multiprogrammed computer the available memory will generally, at any given time, be shared amongst a number of processes, and it is not possible for the individual programmer to know in advance which other programs will be resident in memory when his or her own program is run. This means that the programmer does not know at the time of writing the program precisely where-abouts in memory it will be located, and hence cannot write the program in terms of absolute memory addresses. If the memory allocated to the program remained fixed during its entire run, then it would of course be possible to transform symbolic or relative addresses into absolute addresses at the time the program was loaded, but in fact this is seldom the case. As processes run to completion the space they use becomes free for other processes, and it may be necessary to move processes around in memory in order to make best use of the space available. In particular, it may be desirable to move processes so that small noncontiguous areas of free memory become compacted into a larger, more useful, single area. Thus the region of memory allocated to a process may change during the process's lifetime, and the system must be responsible for transforming the addresses used by the programmer into the actual addresses in which the process is physically located.

(2) Protection

When several processes are sharing memory it is of course essential for their integrity that none of them is permitted to alter the contents of memory locations which are currently allocated to others. Compile time checks on program addresses are an inadequate protection since most languages allow the dynamic calculation of addresses at run time, for example by computing array subscripts or pointers into data structures. Hence all memory references generated by a process must be checked at run time to ensure that they refer only to the memory space allocated to that process. (Strictly speaking, only write accesses need be checked, but if privacy of information is required then read accesses must also be checked.)

(3) Sharing

Despite the need for protection, there are occasions when several processes should be allowed access to the same portion of memory. For example, if a number of processes are executing the same program it is advantageous to allow each process to access the same copy of the program rather than have its own separate copy. Similarly, processes may sometimes need to share a data structure and thus have common access to the area of memory holding it. The memory management system must therefore allow controlled access to shared areas of memory without compromising essential protection.

(4) Logical organisation

The traditional computer has a one-dimensional, or linear, address space in which addresses are numbered sequentially from zero to the upper limit of memory. While this organisation closely mirrors the hardware of the machine it does not really reflect the ways in which programs are usually written. Most programs are structured in some way – into modules or procedures – and refer to distinct areas of modifiable or unmodifiable data. For example, a compiler may be written with separate modules for lexical analysis, syntax analysis, and code generation, and among its data areas may be a table of reserved words (unmodifiable) and a symbol table (modified as new identifiers are encountered during compilation). If the logical divisions into program and data are reflected in a corresponding *segmentation* of address space then several advantages accrue. Firstly, it is possible for segments to be coded independently and for all references from one segment to another to be filled in by the system at run time; secondly, it is possible with little extra overhead to give different degrees of protection (for example, read only, execute only) to different segments; and thirdly, it is possible to introduce mechanisms by which segments can be shared among processes.

(5) Physical organisation

Historically, the general desire for large amounts of storage space and the high cost of fast memory have led to the almost universal adoption of two-level storage systems. The compromise between speed and cost is typically achieved by supplementing a relatively small amount (typically tens of millions of bytes) of direct access main memory by a much larger amount (perhaps several thousand million bytes) of secondary memory, or backing store. Main memory uses semiconductor technology, and has an access time of the order of 70 nanoseconds; backing store is usually based on magnetic discs, with an access time of up to 50 milliseconds.

Since in typical systems only information in main memory can be accessed directly, the organisation of the flow of information between main and secondary memories is obviously of prime importance. It is of course possible to rest the onus of organisation on individual programmers, making them responsible for moving sections of program or data to or from main memory as required. Indeed, in the early days of computing this is what was done, and the technique of *overlay programming* – writing sections of program which overlaid themselves in memory – became an art in itself. However, there are two sound reasons which militate against such an approach. The first is that the programmers do not want to expend a great deal of effort in writing complicated overlays, being too interested in solving their own problems to waste energy on side issues. Clever compilers could help by automatically generating overlay code at appropriate points in the program, but in many cases the compiler does not have sufficient information to know when the overlays will be required. The second reason is that because of dynamic relocation the programmer does not know at the time of writing how much space will be available or whereabouts in memory that space will be. Overlay programming thus becomes impracticable.

It is clear from these arguments that the task of moving information between the two levels of memory should be a system responsibility. How this responsibility can be carried out is discussed later in this chapter.

5.2 Virtual memory

The objectives listed above can be achieved by the conceptually simple (and pleasingly elegant) device of using an address translation mechanism, or *address map*, to transform the addresses used by the programmer into the corresponding physical memory locations actually allocated to the program. The maintenance of the address map is a system function, and possible implementations are discussed in the next section. The crucial point at this stage is the distinction between *program addresses* – addresses used by the programmer – and the physical *memory locations* into which they are mapped.

The range of program addresses is known as the *address space* (or *name space*); the range of memory locations in the computer is the *memory space*. If the address map is denoted by N, and the memory space by M, the address map can be denoted by

$$f : N \rightarrow M$$

On current computers the memory space is generally linear – that is, the memory locations are numbered sequentially from zero – and its size is equal to the amount of main memory included in the configuration (the exception is where part of the main memory is faulty and is temporarily configured out of the system leaving the remaining memory disjoint). We shall see that the address space, however, need not be linear, and depending on the particular implementation of the address map its size may be smaller than, equal to, or larger than that of the memory space.

An alternative way of looking at the address map is to regard it as a means of allowing the programmer to use a range of program addresses which may be quite different from the range of memory locations available. Thus the programmer 'sees', and programs for, a *virtual memory* whose characteristics differ from those of the real memory. The address map is so designed as to produce a virtual memory convenient for the programmer, and so as to achieve some or all of the objectives listed in the previous section. The provision of virtual memory is a good example of the transformation (discussed in chapter 1) of the basic computer into a more convenient virtual machine.

In the next section we shall describe various virtual memories and the address maps which provide them.

5.3 Implementation of virtual memory

(1) Base and limit registers

The first two objectives listed in section 5.1, namely relocation and protection, can be achieved by a fairly simple address map as follows.

When a process is loaded into memory the address of the lowest location used is placed in a *base register* (or *datum register*), and all program addresses are interpreted as being relative to this *base address*. The address map thus consists simply of adding the program address to the base address to produce the corresponding memory location; that is

$$f(a) = B + a$$

where a is the program address, and B is the base address of the process.

Relocation is accomplished by simply moving the process and resetting the base address to the appropriate value. Protection of memory space among processes can be achieved by adding a second register – the *limit register* – which contains the address of the highest location which a particular process is permitted to access. The address map (see figure 5.1) performed by the memory addressing hardware then proceeds according to the following scheme

(a) **if** $a < 0$ **then** memory violation

(b) $a' := B + a$

(c) **if** $a' >$ limit **then** memory violation

(d) a' is required location

It is worth noting that the address space mapped by this scheme is linear, and its size, being the difference between the base and limit registers, is necessarily less than or equal to the size of the memory space. Thus objectives (3) and (4) of section 5.1 are not achieved.

In order that the address mapping operation shall not be prohibitively time consuming, the base and limit registers must be implemented in fast hardware. The cost of the registers can be reduced, and the mapping speeded up, by removing the lower order bits, implying that the size of the address space must be a multiple of 2^n (where n is the number of bits removed).

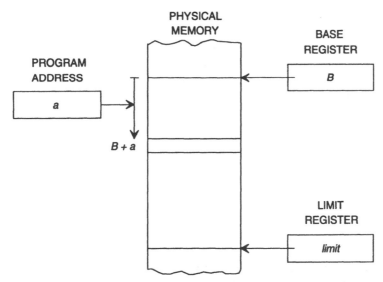

Figure 5.1 Address map for base and limit registers

A slight variation on the base-limit scheme is to use the limit register to hold the *length* of the memory space rather than its upper limit. In this case the address map is

(a) if $a < 0$ or $a >$ *length* **then** memory violation

(b) $a' := B + a$

(c) a' is required location

The advantage is that the limit check does not depend on the result of the addition, so both the checks and the addition can be performed in parallel. (The access is aborted if a memory violation occurs.)

It is impracticable, for economic reasons, to provide a pair of base and limit registers for each process which may be present in memory. Instead, a single pair of registers is provided for each processor, and is loaded with the base and limit addresses of the currently active process. These values form part of the volatile environment of the process and are stored when the process is suspended.

The sharing of re-entrant programs can be effected by providing two pairs of registers rather than one. One pair is used to delimit the memory space occupied by the re-entrant code, and the values in them are common to all processes using the code; the other pair is used to delimit the data areas asso-ciated with the code, and hold different values for each process concerned. Older versions of the DECSystem-10 were an example of a machine employ-ing this technique.

(2) Paging

In the base-limit scheme described above, the size of the address space is necessarily less than or equal to that of the memory space. If we wish to give the programmer a virtual memory which is larger than the available physical memory, thus lifting the burden of writing overlays, then we must devise an address map which apparently abolishes the distinction between main and secondary memory. The concept of the *one-level store*, in which secondary memory is made to appear as an extension of main memory, was first intro-duced on the Atlas computer at Manchester University around 1960, and has since had a profound influence on computer design.

The one level store can be realised by the technique of *paging*, whereby the virtual address space is divided into *pages* of equal size (on Atlas 512 words), and the main memory is similarly divided into *page frames* of the same size. The page frames are shared amongst the processes currently in the system, so that at any time a given process will have a few pages resident in main mem-ory (its *active* pages) and the rest resident in secondary memory (its *inactive* pages). The paging mechanism has two functions

(a) to perform the address mapping operation; that is, to determine which page a program address refers to, and find which page frame, if any, the page currently occupies;

(b) to transfer pages from secondary memory to main memory when required, and to transfer them back to secondary memory when they are no longer being used.

We describe these functions in turn. Although the following descriptions refer to byte numbers, they are equally true for those machines which have individually numbered words; we are interested in the smallest addressable quantity in both cases.

In order to determine which page a program address refers to, the high order bits of the address are interpreted as a page number and the low order bits as the byte number within the page. Thus if the page size is 2^n then the bottom n bits of the address represent the byte number, and the remaining bits the page number. The total number of bits in the address is sufficient to address the entire virtual memory. For example, on a VAX the program address is 32 bits long, giving a virtual memory of 2^{32} bytes; the page size is 512 bytes (2^9), and so the least significant 9 bits represent the byte number and the most significant 23 bits represent the page number. The total number of pages in the virtual memory is therefore 2^{23}, whereas a typical machine might have 2^{16} pages (32 megabytes) of physical memory.

It is worth emphasising that the division of the address into page and byte number is a function of the hardware and is transparent to the programmer, who proceeds as if programming in a large sequential address space.

The address map from page and byte number to physical memory location is made by means of a *page table*, the pth entry of which contains the location p' of the page frame containing page number p. (The possibility that the pth page is not in main memory will be dealt with in a moment.) The byte number, b, is added to p' to obtain the required location (see figure 5.2).

The address map is therefore

$$f(a) = f(p, b) = p' + b$$

where program address a, page number p, and byte number b are related to the page size Z by

p = integral part of (a/Z)

b = remainder of (a/Z)

Since the number of page frames (amount of real memory) allocated to a process will usually be less than the number of pages it actually uses, it is quite possible that a program address will refer to a page which is not currently held in main memory. In this case the corresponding entry in the page table will be empty, and a 'page fault' interrupt is given if an attempt is made to access it. The interrupt causes the paging mechanism to initiate the transfer of the missing page from secondary to main memory and update the page table accordingly. The current process is made unrunnable until the transfer is complete.

The location of the page in secondary memory can be held in a separate table or in the page table itself. In the latter case a 'presence' bit in each page table entry is needed to indicate whether or not the page is present in main memory and whether the address field is to be interpreted as a page frame address or a backing store location.

If no empty page frame exists at the time the page fault occurs then some other page must be moved into secondary memory in order to make room for the incoming page. The choice of which page to swap out in this way is the result of a *page turning algorithm*; we discuss various algorithms in later sections. For the present we remark that information required by the page turning algorithm can be held in a few bits added to each page table entry (the shaded section of figure 5.2). This information might be

(a) how many times the page has been referenced

(b) the time the page was last referenced

(c) whether the page has been written to

This information is usually maintained with assistance from the hardware.

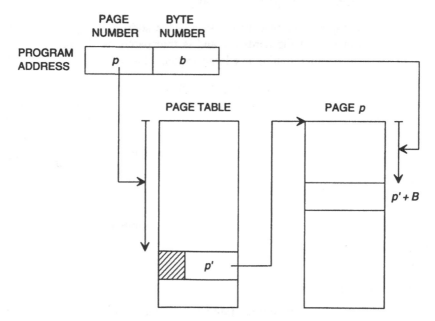

Figure 5.2 Simple address map for paging

It should perhaps be made clear that the entire address mapping operation is performed by the hardware except when a page has to be brought in from secondary memory. In this case the application of the page turning algorithm and the updating of the page table are performed by software.

The foregoing discussion gives a general outline of how paging works; in practice several modifications must be made to obtain a viable implementation. In particular, in the system as described the time required for each memory reference is effectively doubled by the necessity of first accessing the page table. A way of overcoming this would be to keep the page table in a set of fast registers rather than in ordinary memory. However, the size of the page table is proportional to the size of the address space and hence the number of registers required would be too large to be economically feasible. The solution to the problem is to adopt a quite different technique for accessing active pages. This technique involves the addition to the machine of an associative store, which consists of a small set of *page address registers* (PARs), each of which contains the page number of an active page. The PARs have the property that they can be searched *simultaneously* for the page number occurring in a particular program address. For example, in figure 5.3 the program address 3243 is split up into page number 3 and byte number 243. (For convenience the page size is assumed to be 1000.) The page number is then simultaneously compared with the contents of all the PARs, and is found to correspond to that of PAR 5. This indicates that page number 3 currently occupies page frame 5 and so the required memory location is 5243.

The use of an associative store reduces the overhead of the address map by an order of magnitude from that incurred by a page table held in main memory.

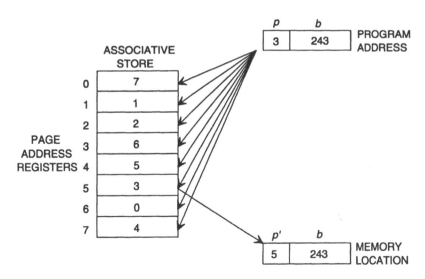

Figure 5.3 Mapping by means of associative store

In order that all active pages should be referenced by a PAR one needs as many PARs as there are page frames in memory. This is possible in systems with small memories, but on larger systems it is not economically feasible to provide all the PARs required. (One might, however, expect that economic arguments will change as technology develops.) In such cases a compromise can be reached by holding a complete page table in memory for each process, and by using a small associative store to reference a few pages of the most recently active processes. In this case the page frame referred to by each PAR is no longer implicit in the PAR's position within the associative store, but must be included as an extra field in the PAR itself. The memory addressing hardware then performs the address mapping operation shown in figure 5.4. As before, software intervention is required only for page replacement.

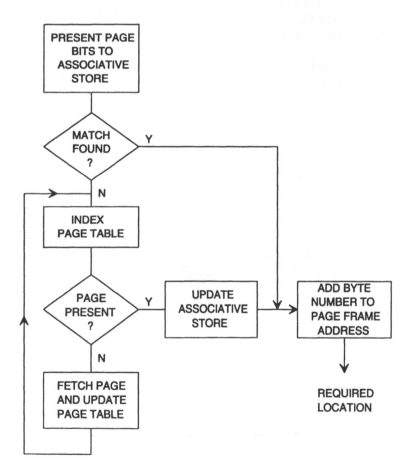

*Figure 5.4 Address mapping operation for paging with
a small associative store*

One problem not illustrated by figure 5.4 is that of distinguishing in the associative store between pages belonging to the current process and pages belonging to other processes. One solution is to extend the PARs to include process identification as well as page number. Each address presented to the associative store must then include the process identification as well as the page bits. An alternative solution is to extend the PARs by a single bit which is set to one in entries belonging to the current process and to zero elsewhere. This solution necessarily implies having a separate associative store for each processor in the configuration. (This is probably advisable in any case in order that the memory addressing logic does not form a bottleneck between processors and memory.)

It is clearly desirable that the associative store contains the page numbers of those pages which are most likely to be referenced. Unfortunately there is no general algorithm for ensuring that this is so (compare section 5.4 on the traffic of pages between main and secondary memories); in practice the associative store is usually filled cyclically with the addresses of the most recently referenced pages. This rather crude algorithm is in fact quite effective; depending on memory size a store of only 8 or 16 registers can be expected to give an average hit rate of better than 99 per cent.

In some machines (for example, the Intel 80486) all of the logic and storage for the implementation of the associative store is included on the CPU chip, with consequent improvement in performance.

It is also important to note that any change made to a page table by the operating system must be reflected in any corresponding entry in the associative store. Privileged instructions are thus provided which will remove all reference to a given page from the associative store or (less commonly) update the associative store copy of the page details.

As a final observation on the mechanics of paging it is worth pointing out the large amount of main memory which can be occupied by the page tables themselves. For example on the DEC VAX the address space consists of 8,388,608 pages of 512 bytes each. This would require 32 megabytes of memory, using 4 bytes per page table entry! A more realistic example on the same machine might be a process using 5 megabytes (10,240 pages) of virtual memory; this would still need 40,960 bytes (80 pages) for its page tables. This problem is tackled by placing the page tables in a separate part of virtual memory (known on the VAX as *system space*) and paging the page tables themselves. More modern machines use larger pages; since each page needs the same amount of space for a page table entry no matter what its size, the net result is to reduce the memory occupied by the page tables. For example, the XA variant of the IBM 370 series uses pages which are 4096 bytes in length, as does the Intel 80486; this reflects to some degree the tendency for more modern machines to have larger main memories.

The size of page tables can be reduced to the number of pages actually used, rather than the number in the address space, by accessing them by hashing rather than by indexing. The idea is that instead of containing an entry for every page in the address space the page table refers only to those pages which have been used. Each time a new page is brought into main memory the page number and corresponding page frame address are entered in the table at a point determined by a suitable hash function. The same hash function can then be used to locate the page during the address mapping operation. The penalty paid for the reduction in size of the page table is an increase in memory access time for some references. The increase is due to two factors: first there is the time required to compute the hash function itself, and second, in the case that the hashed entries in the page table collide, it may be necessary to access the table more than once before the required page is located. Despite this the scheme can be made viable by using an associative store, which can reduce the number of occasions on which the page table is referenced to about one per cent of the total, and by performing the hashing operation by hardware.

(3) Segmentation

The third objective of section 5.1, namely the organisation of address space to reflect logical divisions in program and data, can be achieved by using the technique of *segmentation*. The idea is that the address space is divided into *segments*, each segment corresponding to a procedure, program module, or collection of data. This can be done in a simple way by adding several pairs of base and limit registers to each processor so that the address space can be demarcated into several areas. For example, the Modular One computer had three pairs of registers, and the three segments were used respectively for program, data private to a process, and data shared between processes. The disadvantages of this simple mechanism are that the number of segments is for economic reasons necessarily small, and that there needs to be a convention as to which segments are used for what purpose.

A more flexible arrangement of virtual memory is to allow the programmer to use a large number of segments according to his wishes, and to reference the segments by names assigned by himself. The address space thus becomes two-dimensional, since individual program addresses are identified by giving both a segment name and an address within the segment. (In fact for convenience of implementation the operating system replaces the segment name by a unique segment number when the segment is first referenced.) A generalised program address therefore consists of a pair (s,a), where s is the segment number and a is the address within the segment.

The address map can be implemented by means of a *segment table* for each process, the sth entry of which contains the base location and length of the sth segment of the process. The segment table entries are sometimes referred to as *segment descriptors.* In simplified form the mapping operation is (see figure 5.5)

(a) extract program address (s,a)

(b) use s to index segment table

(c) **if** $a < 0$ **or** $a > l$ **then** memory violation

(d) $(b+a)$ is the required memory location

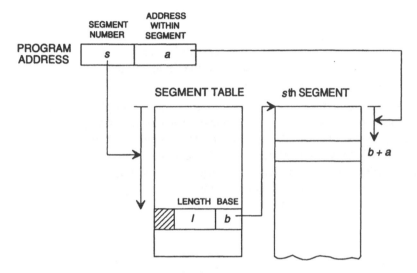

Figure 5.5 Simple address map for segmentation

Protection against memory violation is provided by comparing the byte address with the segment length l. Additional protection may be given by incorporating into each segment descriptor a number of *protection bits* (shown shaded in figure 5.5) which specify the modes in which the corresponding segment can be accessed.

Note that a segment may readily be shared by a number of processes. All that is needed is a descriptor for the segment concerned in the segment table of each process. The protection bits in each descriptor may be different, so that, for example, one process may have read-only access to a shared segment while another process is able to write into it. Thus segmentation allows flexible sharing of programs and data among processes.

It is worth emphasising that despite the apparent similarity between figures 5.2. and 5.5 the address maps for paging and segmentation are quite different in the following respects.

(a) The purpose of segmentation is the logical division of address space; the purpose of paging is the physical division of memory to implement a one level store.

(b) Pages are of a fixed size determined by the machine architecture; segments can be of any size determined by the user (up to a limit fixed by the way in which the program address is partitioned into segment and byte numbers).

(c) The division of the program address into page and byte numbers is a function of the hardware, and overflow of the byte number automatically increments the page number; the division into segment and byte numbers is a logical one, and there is no overflow from byte number to segment number. (If the byte number overflows then a memory violation is generated.)

In practice the address mapping operation is not as simple as the foregoing description suggests. The major complication is that for large programs it may not be possible to hold all segments in main memory, particularly since the memory will be shared between several processes. This is effectively a situation in which the virtual memory is larger than the physical memory, and it can be treated either by employing paging or by swapping entire segments in and out of memory as required.

When paging is employed each segment generally consists of several pages and has its own page table. Provided that some of the segment's pages are in memory, the segment table entry points to the segment's page table; otherwise, it is empty. The address mapping operation performed by the addressing hardware is as follows.

(a) Extract program address (s,a)

(b) Use s to index segment table

(c) If sth entry is empty then create a new (empty) page table, otherwise extract address of page table

(d) Split byte address a into page number p and byte number b

(e) Use p to index page table

(f) If pth entry is empty then fetch page from backing store, otherwise extract page frame address p'

(g) Add p' to byte number b to obtain required location.

Steps (a) to (c) represent the mapping due to segmentation; steps (d) to (g) (which correspond to figure 5.2) represent the mapping due to paging the segments.

The extra memory references required to access the segment and page tables can be avoided by the use of an associative store in a way similar to that described earlier for paging alone. In this case each entry in the associative store contains both the segment and page numbers of the most recently accessed pages. The segment and page bits of each program address are presented to the associative store (figure 5.6) and if a match is found the byte number is added to the corresponding page frame address to obtain the required memory location. Only when no match is found is the full operation described earlier invoked.

If paging is not employed then segment table entries are as shown in figure 5.5. A segment fault causes the whole of the required segment to be brought into main memory; some other segment may have to be relegated to backing store to create sufficient space. Policies for allocating memory among segments will be described in the next section.

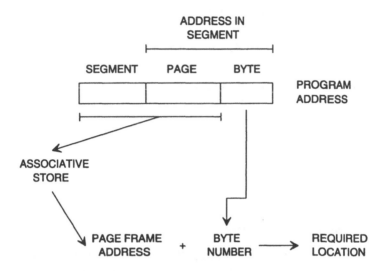

Figure 5.6 Address mapping operation for paged
segments using associative store

The advantages of using paging to implement a segmented address space are twofold. Firstly, the entire segment need not be present in main memory – only those pages currently in use need be accommodated; secondly, it is not necessary that the pages occupy contiguous areas of memory – they can be dispersed throughout memory wherever a suitable page frame is found. Against paging must be set the complexity of the address map and the overhead of the page tables. Examples of systems which support paged segments are the Honeywell 645, the ICL 2900 and large IBM 370s; those which have unpaged segments include the large Burroughs machines (for example, the B6700) and the larger PDP11s. The Intel 80486 will also support paged segments in one of its several operating modes; in fact it has a paging unit and a segmentation unit, each of which can be enabled separately, thus allowing normal paging (as mentioned in (2)), or segmentation with and without paging.

5.4 Memory allocation policies

The discussions in the last section were concerned exclusively with the *mechanisms* of memory management rather than with the *policies* governing them. In this section we shall concentrate on the policies which enable the mechanisms to be put to good use.

Policies for managing memory fall into three broad categories.

(1) *Replacement policies*, which determine what information is to be removed from main memory, that is, create unallocated regions of memory.

(2) *Fetch policies*, which determine when information is to be loaded into main memory, for example on demand or in advance.

(3) *Placement policies*, which determine where information is to be placed in main memory, that is choose a subset of some unallocated region.

We shall see that policies of type (2) are very much the same for both paged and non-paged systems. Policies of types (1) and (3), however, differ between paged and non-paged systems: the differences arise from the fixed size of pages as opposed to the variable sizes of the blocks of information which have to be handled in non-paged systems.

(1) Placement policies for non-paged systems

In this subsection we are considering the transfer of information into main memory in the cases where the virtual address space is either segmented or implemented by base-limit pairs. In either case we shall denote the blocks of information which are being transferred by the word 'segment', with the understanding that if a single base-limit system is being used then a segment will be the entire address space of a process.

The situation is that from time to time segments are inserted into or deleted from the main memory. (The insertions and deletions occur on invocations of the fetch and replacement policies respectively.) If the system is in equilibrium, (that is, over a period of time the space freed by deletion is equal to that filled by insertion) then the memory has the chequer-board appearance of figure 5.7.

It is clear that the placement policy must maintain a list of the locations and sizes of all unallocated 'holes'; we shall call this the *hole list*. Its task is to decide which hole to use, and to update the hole list after each insertion. If the

Figure 5.7 Segmented memory

segment to be placed is smaller than the hole to be used, then the segment is placed at the 'left hand' or 'bottom end' of the hole. This tactic minimises the amount by which the hole is fragmented. If, on the other hand, the segment is larger than any available hole then the placement policy has the additional task of moving around the segments already in memory to create a hole large enough for its purpose.

Numerous placement algorithms are described in the literature, for example Knuth (1973); we shall give four principal ones here. In each case the sizes of the holes are denoted by $x_1, x_2, ..., x_n$.

(a) Best fit

The holes are listed in order of increasing size, that is

$$x_1 \leq x_2 \leq ... \leq x_n$$

If s is the size of the segment to be placed, then find the smallest i such that

$$s \leq x_i$$

(b) Worst fit

The holes are listed in order of decreasing size, that is

$$x_1 \geq x_2 \geq ... \geq x_n$$

Place the segment in the first hole, and link the hole formed by the remaining space back into the appropriate position in the list.

(c) First fit

The holes are listed in order of increasing base address. Find the smallest i such that $s \leq x_i$. The use of the algorithm leads, after a time, to an accumulation of small holes near the head of the list. To avoid excessive search time for large segments the start position can be advanced cyclically by one element after each search.

(d) Buddy

For this algorithm segment sizes must be powers of 2, that is $s = 2^i$ for some i less than a maximum k. A separate list is maintained for holes of each size 2^1, 2^2, ..., 2^k. A hole may be removed from the $(i + 1)$-list by splitting it in half, thereby creating a pair of 'buddies' of size 2^i on the i-list. Conversely a pair of buddies may be removed from the i-list, coalesced, and put on the $(i + 1)$-list. The algorithm for finding a hole of size 2^i is recursive

> **procedure** get hole(i);
> **begin if** $i = k + 1$ **then** failure;
>   **if** i-list empty **then begin** get hole($i + 1$);
>   split hole into buddies;
>   put buddies on i-list
>   **end**;
>   take first hole in i-list
> **end**;

To the more suspicious reader it may appear strange that algorithms (a) and (b) are both viable since they adopt directly opposing strategies regarding the ordering of the hole list. Algorithm (a) is perhaps the more intuitively appealing since it appears to minimise the wastage in each hole it selects (that is, it selects the smallest hole that will do the job). Algorithm (b), however, works on the philosophy that making an allocation from a large hole is likely to leave a hole large enough to be useful in future, whereas making an allocation from a small hole will leave an even smaller hole which will probably be quite useless.

A problem common to all the placement policies described is *fragmentation* – the splitting up of free memory into holes so small that new segments cannot be fitted in. When this occurs some *compaction* of memory is necessary; that is, all segments must be moved downwards so that a single large hole appears at the top of memory. Compaction is most easily achieved if the holes are listed in address order, as in the first-fit algorithm. An alternative approach is to compact memory every time a segment is removed, thus avoiding fragmentation altogether; the overhead of frequent compaction is offset by not having to search a hole list whenever a segment is to be placed.

(2) Placement policies for paged systems

Placement policies for paged systems are far simpler than for non-paged systems; to place k pages we simply use a replacement policy to free k page frames. Fragmentation, in the sense described for non-paged systems, cannot occur, since all pages and page frames are of equal size. However, a paged system can suffer from a different form of fragmentation, *internal fragmentation*, which arises because the space required by a process is not an exact multiple of the page size. Consequently a part of the last page frame allocated is generally wasted; the average wastage can be expected to be half the page size. If the address space consists of several paged segments, the degree of internal fragmentation is multiplied by the number of segments currently held in main memory.

(3) Replacement policies for paged systems

The job of a replacement policy is to decide which blocks of information to relegate to secondary memory when space has to be found in main memory for new blocks. In this subsection we consider the case where the blocks of information are pages; we shall see later that the same policies can be applied, with appropriate modifications, in the non-paged situation.

Ideally one wants to replace the page which is not going to be referenced for the longest time in the future. Unfortunately, knowledge of the future is hard to come by: the best one can do is infer from past behaviour what future behaviour is likely to be. The accuracy of the inference depends on the predictability of program behaviour, which we shall discuss further in the section on fetch policies.

Three common replacement algorithms are

(a) Least recently used (LRU)

'Replace the page which has least recently been used.' The assumption is that future behaviour will closely follow recent behaviour. The overhead is that of recording the sequence of access to all pages.

(b) Least frequently used (LFU)

'Replace the page which has been used least frequently during some immediately preceding time interval.' The justification is similar to (a), and the overhead is that of keeping a 'use count' for each page. One drawback is that a recently loaded page will in general have a low use count and may be replaced inadvisedly. A way to avoid this is to inhibit the replacement of pages loaded within the last time interval.

(c) First in, first out (FIFO)

'Replace the page which has been resident longest.' This is a simpler algorithm, whose overhead is only that of recording the loading sequence of pages. It ignores the possibility that the oldest page may be the most heavily referenced.

Simulation studies have shown a difference in performance of the three algorithms (in terms of the number of transfers required during the running of a number of jobs) which varies according to the number of jobs being run, but which is rarely more than 15 per cent. Algorithm (c) gives a generally poorer performance than the other two.

Finally, it is worth noting that pages which have not been written to need not be transferred back to secondary memory provided that a copy already exists there. A record of whether a particular page has been written to can be kept in a single bit in the corresponding page table entry.

(4) Replacement policies for non-paged systems

In this subsection we consider policies for the situation where the blocks of information to be replaced are segments in the broad sense defined in (1) earlier.

The major objective is the same as for paged systems – that is, to replace the segment which is least likely to be referenced in the immediate future. One might therefore expect the same policies to be applicable, and this is indeed the case, but with one major qualification. The qualification arises from the fact that not all segments occupy equal amounts of memory, so consideration of which segment to relegate to secondary memory is influenced by the size of the segment to be placed. If a small segment is to be brought into main memory then only a small segment need be replaced; on the other hand, the placement of a large segment requires the replacement of another large segment (or several smaller ones).

Possibly the simplest algorithm is to replace the single segment (if one exists) which, together with any adjacent holes, will free enough space for the incoming segment. If there are several such segments, then one of the policies discussed earlier, such as LRU, can be used to discriminate between them. If no single segment is large enough to create sufficient space, then several segments have to be replaced: a possible choice is the smallest set of contiguous segments which will free the space required.

The danger with such an algorithm is that the segment (or segments) replaced, being selected mainly on criteria of size, may be referenced again shortly afterwards. The danger can be reduced by selecting segments purely on (say) an LRU basis, but since the selected segments are not likely to be contiguous some compaction of memory will be required. The reader will readily appreciate that the relative emphasis given to segment size, expectation of future reference, and compaction, can produce a variety of complex algorithms which are difficult to assess except in practice. We shall not pursue the subject further here, but refer the interested reader to more detailed studies such as Knuth (1973) and Denning (1970).

(5) Fetch policies

Fetch policies determine when to move a block of information from secondary to main memory. The arguments for choosing a policy are roughly the same whether the blocks are pages or segments (in the broad sense that we have been using). Fetch policies are divided into two broad classes: *demand* and *anticipatory*. Demand policies fetch blocks when they are needed; anticipatory policies fetch them in advance.

Demand policies are clearly the easier to implement – a missing block (segment or page) fault generates a fetch request, and the placement and/or replacement policies allocate memory for the new block. In non-paged systems (for example, Burroughs machines) the transfer of blocks is usually on demand, as it is on some paged machines (for example Atlas).

Anticipatory policies rely on predictions of future program behaviour in order to be fully effective. Prediction can be based on two things

(a) the nature of construction of programs

(b) inference from a process's past behaviour

Consider (a) for a moment. Many programs exhibit behaviour known as *operating in context*; that is, in any small time interval a program tends to operate within a particular logical module, drawing its instructions from a single procedure and its data from a single data area. Thus program references tend to be grouped into small localities of address space. The locality of reference is strengthened by the frequent occurrence of looping; the tighter the loop, the smaller the spread of references. The observation of this behaviour leads to the postulation (Denning, 1970) of the so-called *principle of locality*: program references tend to be grouped into small localities of address space, and these localities tend to change only intermittently.

The validity of the principle of locality will vary from program to program; it will, for example, be more valid for programs making sequential array accesses than for programs accessing complex data structures. The principle is used by Denning in the context of paged memory to formulate the *working set* model of program behaviour which we briefly describe in the next section.

An important point to remember is that pages or segments within a virtual address space do not generally occupy any space (either in secondary or main memory) until they are used. The only overhead in having a large virtual address space is the size of the page or segment tables involved; these generally have to exist, although there are sometimes ways of minimising them, depending on the hardware in use.

5.5 The working set model

The working set model of program behaviour (Denning, 1968 and 1980) is an attempt to establish a framework for understanding the performance of paging systems in a multiprogramming environment. The policies for memory management which we discussed in the last section are based on a study of how processes behave in isolation; they do not take into account any effects which may arise from having several processes in the machine at once. The competition for memory space between processes can in fact lead to behaviour which would not occur if each process ran separately.

As an illustration of what can happen, consider a single processor system with a paged memory in which the degree of multiprogramming (that is, the number of processes present in memory) is steadily increased. As the degree of multiprogramming rises one might expect that the processor utilisation would also rise, since the dispatcher would always have a greater chance of finding a process to run. Indeed observation confirms that this is generally the case, so long as the degree of multiprogramming is kept below a certain level which is dependent on the size of memory available. However, if the degree of multiprogramming exceeds this level then it is found (see figure 5.8) that there is a marked increase in the paging traffic between main and secondary memories accompanied by a sudden decrease in processor utilisation. The explanation for this is that the high degree of multiprogramming makes it impossible for every process to keep sufficient pages in memory to avoid generating a large number of page faults. This means that the backing store channel can become saturated, that most processes are blocked awaiting a page transfer, and that the processor is under-utilised. This state of affairs is referred to by the descriptive term *thrashing*.

The lesson to be learned from this illustration is that each process requires a certain minimum number of pages, called its *working set*, to be held in main memory before it can effectively use the central processor. If less than this number are present then the process is continually interrupted by page faults which contribute towards thrashing. For thrashing to be avoided the degree of multiprogramming must be no greater than the level at which the working sets of all processes can be held in main memory.

The question now arises of how to determine which pages constitute the working set of a process. The answer is to inspect the process's recent history and to appeal to the principle of locality mentioned in the last section. More formally, the working set of a process at time t is defined to be

$$w(t, h) = \{ \text{ page } i \mid \text{page } i \in N \text{ and page } i \text{ appears in the last } h \text{ references} \}$$

In other words the working set is the set of pages which have recently been referred to, 'recentness' being one of the parameters (h) of the set. From the principle of locality one would expect the working set to change membership

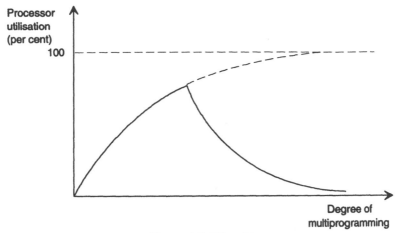

Figure 5.8 Thrashing

slowly in time. Denning has shown that the expected size $w(h)$ of the working set varies with h as shown in figure 5.9.

As h is increased (that is, the further into the past one looks), the fewer extra pages one expects to find in the working set. This enables one to establish a reasonably small value for h (for example h_0) in the knowledge that a larger value of h would not significantly increase the working set size.

So far as fetch and replacement policies are concerned the value of the working set lies in the following rule:

> Run a process only if its entire working set is in main memory, and never remove a page which is part of the working set of some process.

Although the working sets of some processes may be rather arbitrarily defined, and although the principle of locality does not apply to some programs, application of the above rule can make a significant contribution towards the prevention of thrashing. The working set model is widely used, though the definition of working set varies somewhat from one operating system to another.

It is important to realise that the rule given above is more than a pure memory management policy since it implies a correlation between memory allocation and processor allocation. So far in this chapter we have treated memory management as an issue distinct from the management of other resources. In practice management of a single resource cannot always be divorced from consideration of other resources, but we shall defer a full treatment of resource allocation until chapter 8.

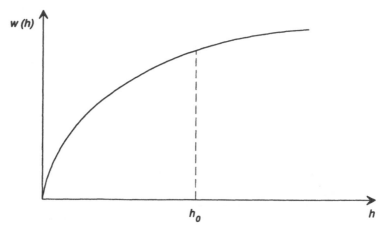

Figure 5.9 Expected size of the working set

5.6 Implementation in the paper system

It may appear to the reader that the memory management policies discussed in this chapter have a rather *ad hoc* air, and that the choice of algorithm in a particular case is somewhat arbitrary. To a certain extent this is true; many of the policies are founded on common sense and experience, backed up in some cases by analytical or statistical justification. A powerful aid in the choice of algorithm is simulation; ideally each option should be tested with a simulation of the job mix expected. Some studies are reported by Knuth (1973), and an extensive bibliography is given by Denning (1970).

In order to implement in our paper operating system the mechanisms of section 5.3 we add to the volatile environment of each process

(a) a copy of the contents of the base and limit registers

or

(b) a pointer to its segment table

or

(c) a pointer to its page table

depending on the architecture of our machine.

If we have a non-paged machine then we introduce the hole list as a further data structure pointed to from the central table. The memory management layer of our system consists of code to implement the policies discussed in section 5.4.

Our system has now reached the stage shown in figure 5.10.

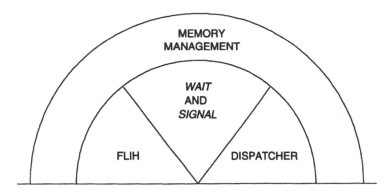

Figure 5.10 Current state of the paper operating system

6 Input and Output

At this stage in the development of our paper operating system, we have established an environment in which processes can exist and in which memory can be allocated to hold the associated programs and data. We now turn our attention to the means by which processes communicate with the outside world: that is, to mechanisms for the input and output of information.

Traditionally, I/O is regarded as one of the more sordid areas of operating system design in that it is a field in which generalisation is difficult and *ad hoc* methods abound. The reason for this is the wide variety of peripheral devices employed; a particular configuration may include devices which differ greatly in their characteristics and mode of operation. Specifically, devices may differ on one or more of the following counts.

(1) Speed

There may be a difference of several orders of magnitude between the data transfer rates of various devices. A magnetic disk, for instance, may be able to transfer 10^{12} characters per second, compared with a terminal keyboard speed of only a few characters per second (depending on the typist!).

(2) Unit of transfer

Data may be transferred in units of characters, words, bytes, blocks or records, according to the peripheral used.

(3) Data representation

Data may be encoded in different ways on different I/O media. Even on a single medium, such as magnetic tape, several different codes may be employed.

(4) Permissible operations

Devices differ in the kind of operation they can perform. One example is the obvious distinction between input and output; another is the ability to rewind magnetic tape but not printer paper.

(5) Error conditions

Failure to complete a data transfer may have various causes such as a hardware detected data error, a printer that has run out of paper, or a checksum error, depending on the peripheral being used.

Clearly the diversity exemplified above is difficult to handle in a uniform manner. However we shall attempt in this chapter to construct a framework for an I/O system in which device-dependent characteristics are isolated so far as possible and in which some degree of uniformity is achieved. We start by considering some design objectives and their implications.

6.1 Design objectives and implications

(1) Character code independence

It is obviously undesirable that in order to write programs a user should require detailed knowledge of the character codes used by various peripherals. The I/O system must take responsibility for recognising different character codes and for presenting data to user programs in a standard form.

(2) Device independence

There are two aspects to device independence. First, a program should be independent of the particular device of a given type which it happens to be allocated. For example, it should not matter in which compact disk drive a particular disk is inserted, or which printer is used for a program's output. Device independence of this kind ensures that a program does not fail simply because a particular device is broken or allocated elsewhere. It gives the operating system the freedom to allocate a device of the appropriate type according to overall availability at the time.

Second, and more demanding, it is desirable that programs should so far as possible be independent of the device type used for their I/O. Clearly device independence of this nature cannot be carried as far as sending output to an input device; what we have in mind is that only minimal changes to a job should be required for it to receive its data from disk rather than (say) a cassette of magnetic tape.

(3) Efficiency

Since I/O operations often form a bottleneck in a computing system it is desirable to perform them as efficiently as possible.

(4) Uniform treatment of devices

In the interests of simplicity and freedom from error it is desirable to handle all devices in a uniform manner. For reasons already mentioned this may be difficult in practice.

Some implications of these objectives are immediately apparent. First, character code independence implies the existence of a uniform internal representation of all characters. This representation is called the *internal character code*, and translation mechanisms must be associated with each peripheral to perform the appropriate conversions on input and output. For peripherals which may handle a variety of character codes, a separate translation mechanism must be supplied for each code supported. Translation is performed immediately on input and immediately before output, so that only those processes intimately connected with peripheral handling need be aware of anything but the standard internal code. The translation mechanism will generally be a table, or in some cases a short piece of program.

Next, device independence implies that programs should operate not on actual devices but on virtual devices, variously called *streams*, *files* (MULTICS and UNIX) or *data sets* (IBM). The streams are used within a program without any reference to physical devices; the programmer merely directs output and input to or from particular streams. The association of streams with real devices is usually made by the operating system on the basis of information supplied by the user (via operating system commands). The way in which the user specifies this information will be discussed further in chapter 11; for our present purpose it is sufficient to show an example (from VMS) of such a specification, as follows.

DEFINE OUTPUT1 TAPE0:

meaning that a stream called OUTPUT1 is to be bound to magnetic tape drive 0. In many cases it is possible to specify only the type of device required, leaving the operating system the freedom to associate the stream with any available device of the required type. Independence of device type is achieved with a trivial change to the specification (for example, output to disk might be obtained by changing TAPE0 to DISK0). The equivalence of streams and device types for a particular process can be recorded in a list of stream descriptors pointed to from its process descriptor (see figure 6.1); the allocation of a particular device of a given type is made when the process first uses the corresponding stream. We say that at this point the process *opens* the stream; the stream is *closed* (indicating that it is no longer to be used), either explicitly by the process or implicitly when the process terminates. For the process shown in figure 6.1, terminal 3 has been defined as input stream 1, printer 2 has been defined as output stream 2, and output stream 1, which has not yet been opened, is to be a magnetic tape drive.

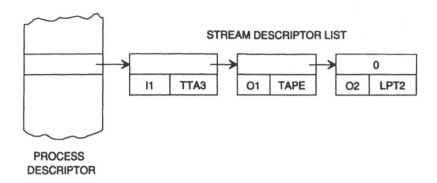

STREAM DESCRIPTOR LIST

| | I1 | TTA3 | | O1 | TAPE | | O2 | LPT2 |

PROCESS
DESCRIPTOR

Figure 6.1 Device and stream information for a process

A third implication of our design objectives is that the I/O system should be constructed in such a way that device characteristics are clearly associated with the devices themselves rather then with the routines which handle them (the *device handlers*). In this way it is possible for device handlers to show great similarities, and for their differences of operation to derive solely from parametric information obtained from the characteristics of the particular device concerned. The necessary isolation of device characteristics can be achieved by encoding them in a *device descriptor* associated with each device, and by using the descriptor as a source of information for the device handler. The characteristic information about a device which may be stored in its descriptor is

(1) the device identification

(2) the instructions which operate the device

(3) pointers to character translation tables

(4) the current status: whether the device is busy, free or broken

(5) the current user process: a pointer to the process descriptor of the process, if any, which is currently using the device

All device descriptors can be linked together in a *device structure* which is pointed to from the central table.

Lastly, it is difficult to achieve fully uniform treatment of devices when they may have widely differing characteristics. One approach, used in UNIX, is to treat all devices as if they are files. (We describe files in more detail in the next chapter.) Every device has a name which is indistinguishable from a file name, and all reasonable operations are permissible on such *special files*. For example, a printer might have the name */dev/lp*, and it would be possible simply to issue a command to copy the contents of a data file to this special file; the effect would be to print the contents of the file. However, it would be unreasonable to expect success in any attempt to copy anything *from* the special file for such a device; this would be equivalent to attempting input from a clearly output-only device. There are other limitations with this approach; while reading and writing are obvious operations, other mechanisms are needed for further device control (for example, rewinding a magnetic tape). UNIX achieves this by providing methods for transfer of control information to and from special files, using secondary forms of the normal read and write operations.

6.2 The I/O procedures

In the last section we made significant progress towards the uniform treatment of devices by isolating all device dependent characteristics in the device descriptors. We are now in a position to consider how the operating system handles a request for I/O from a user process.

A typical request from a process will be a call to the operating system of the general form

DOIO(*stream, mode, amount, destination, semaphore*)

where

DOIO	is the name of a system I/O procedure
stream	is the number of the stream on which I/O is to take place
mode	indicates what operation, such as data transfer or rewind, is required; it may also indicate, if relevant, what character code is to be used
amount	is the amount of data to be transferred, if any
destination	(or *source*) is the location into which (or from which) the transfer, if any, is to occur
semaphore	is the address of a semaphore *request serviced* which is to be signalled when the I/O operation is complete.

The I/O procedure DOIO is re-entrant, which means that it may be used by several processes at once, keeping track of the state of each separately. Its function is to map the stream number to the appropriate physical device, to check the consistency of the parameters supplied to it, and to initiate service of the request.

The first of these operations is straightforward. The device which corresponds to the specified stream is determined from the information placed in the stream descriptor list of the calling process at the time the stream was opened (see figure 6.1). Once the device is identified, the parameters of the I/O request can be checked for consistency against the information held in the device

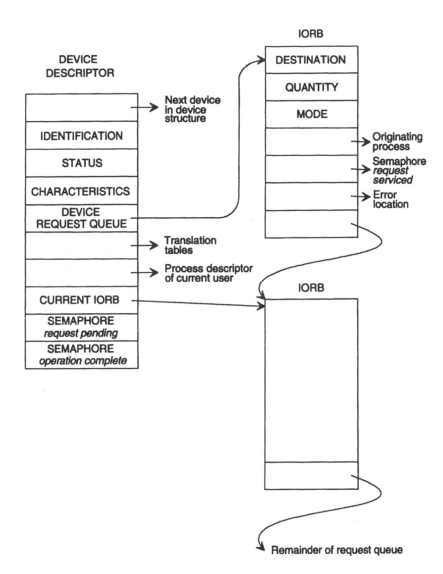

Figure 6.2 Device descriptor and device request queue

descriptor, and if an error is detected an exit can be made to the caller. One particular check which may be performed is that the device is capable of operating in the desired mode, and another is that the size and destination of the data transfer correspond to the mode of operation. In the case of input devices which can transfer only single characters, the specified quantity of data must be 1, and the destination either a register or memory location; for input devices which transfer blocks of data directly to memory the specified quantity must be equal to the block size (fixed or variable according to the device) and the destination the memory location at which the transfer is to start. Similar considerations apply to output devices.

When the checks have been completed the I/O procedure assembles the parameters of the request into an *I/O request block* (IORB) which it adds to a queue of similar blocks which represent other requests for use of the same device. These other requests may come from the same process, or, in the case of a shared device such as a disk, from other processes. The *device request queue* is attached to the descriptor of the device concerned (see figure 6.2), and is serviced by a separate process called a *device handler* which we shall describe in the next section. The I/O procedure notifies the device handler that it has placed a request on the queue by signalling a semaphore *request pending,* associated with the device and contained in the device descriptor. Similarly, once the I/O operation is complete the device handler notifies the user process by means of the semaphore *request serviced* (whose address was a parameter of the I/O procedure and was passed to the device handler as an element of the IORB). This semaphore can be initialised either by the user process or by the I/O procedure when the IORB is created.

The complete I/O routine is

> **procedure** DOIO(*stream, mode, amount, destination, semaphore*);
> **begin** look up device in process descriptor;
>   check parameters against device characteristics;
>   **if** error **then** error exit;
>   construct IORB;
>   add IORB to device request queue;
>   *signal*(*request pending*)
> **end**;

6.3 The device handlers

As mentioned in the last section, a device handler is a process which is responsible for servicing the requests on a device request queue and for notifying the originating process when the service has been completed. There is a separate handler for each device, but since all handlers operate in a similar way they can make use of shareable programs. Any differences in behaviour between handlers are derived from the characteristics stored in the descriptors of the particular devices.

A device handler operates in a continuous cycle during which it removes an IORB from the request queue, initiates the corresponding I/O operation, waits for the operation to be completed, and notifies the originating process. The complete cycle for an input operation is

```
repeat indefinitely
begin wait(request pending);
        pick an IORB from request queue;
        extract details of request;
        initiate I/O operation;
        wait(operation complete);
        if error then plant error information;
        translate character(s) if necessary;
        transfer data to destination;
        signal(request serviced);
        delete IORB
end;
```

The following notes, which should be read with reference to figure 6.2, may clarify the details.

(1) The semaphore *request pending*, contained in the device descriptor, is signalled by the I/O procedure each time it places an IORB on the request queue for this device. If the queue is empty the semaphore is zero and the device handler is suspended.

(2) The device handler may pick an IORB from the queue according to any desired priority algorithm. A first come, first served algorithm is usually adequate, but the handler could be influenced by priority information placed in the IORB by the I/O procedure. In the case of a disk the device handler may service requests in an order which minimises head movements.

(3) The instructions to initiate the I/O operation can be extracted from the device characteristics held in the device descriptor.

(4) The semaphore *operation complete* is signalled by the interrupt routine after an interrupt is generated for this device. The outline program of the interrupt routine, which is entered from the first level interrupt handler, is

```
locate device descriptor;
signal(operation complete);
```

The semaphore *operation complete* is held in the device descriptor. Note that the interrupt routine is very short; all housekeeping is performed by the device handler, which operates in user mode as a normal process.

(5) The error check is made by interrogating the device status when the operation is complete. If there has been an error, such as hardware detected data error, printer out of paper, or even end of file, information about it is deposited in an *error location* whose address is included by the I/O procedure in the IORB.

(6) Character translation is made according to the mode specified in the IORB and the tables pointed to by the device descriptor.

(7) The cycle shown above is for an input operation. In the case of an output operation, the extraction of data from its source and any character translation occur before the operation rather than after.

(8) The address of the semaphore *request serviced* is passed to the device handler as a component of the IORB. It is supplied by the process requesting I/O, as a parameter of the I/O procedure.

The synchronisation and flow of control between the process requesting I/O, the I/O procedure, and the appropriate device handler and interrupt routine are summarised in figure 6.3. Solid arrows represent transfers of control; broken arrows represent synchronisation by means of semaphores. It is important to note that in the scheme illustrated the requesting process proceeds asynchronously with the device handler so that it may perform other computations or make other I/O requests while the original request is being serviced. The requesting process need be held up only on occasions when the I/O operation is incomplete when it executes *wait(request serviced)*.

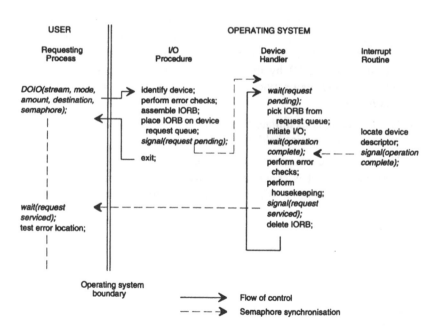

Figure 6.3 Sketch of the I/O system

The disadvantage of this arrangement is that the requesting process must take responsibility for synchronising its actions with those of the device handler. It must not, for example, attempt to use input data which have not yet been provided. This means that the author of the process must be aware that I/O operations are not instantaneous and must be capable of achieving the desired synchronisation by appropriate use of the semaphore *request serviced*.

An alternative arrangement is to place the responsibility for synchronisation within the I/O procedure, which is part of the operating system. This can be done by making the semaphore *request serviced* local to the I/O procedure (that is, its address need no longer be supplied by the requesting process) and by inserting the operations

> *wait(request serviced)*;
> test error location;

in the I/O procedure immediately before its exit. The delay implicit in an I/O operation is now hidden within the operating system; so far as the requesting process is concerned the operation is instantaneous in the sense that when the next instruction after the request is obeyed the operation can be assumed to be complete. To put it another way, the requesting process is executing on a virtual machine in which I/O operations are achieved by a single instantaneous instruction.

The two possible arrangements discussed above may be summarised as follows. In the first the user has the freedom to continue in parallel with the I/O operation but has the responsibility of detecting its completion; in the second the responsibility is taken away but the user also loses the freedom. A good example of the first is to be found in VMS; an example of the second is the I/O system used in UNIX.

6.4 Buffering

The description of the I/O procedure and the device handlers given above assumes that all data transfers are unbuffered. That is, each I/O request from a process causes a physical transfer to occur on the appropriate peripheral. If the process is performing repeated transfers on the same stream it will repeatedly be suspended (on *wait(request serviced)*) while the transfers take place. In order to avoid heavy overheads in process switching it is sometimes convenient to perform I/O transfers in advance of requests being made, thus ensuring that data is available when required. This technique is known as *buffering*.

Input transfers are made by the operating system into an area of memory called an *input buffer*; the user process takes its data from the buffer and is forced to wait only when the buffer becomes empty. When this occurs the operating system refills the buffer and the process continues. Similarly, output transfers from a process are directed to an *output buffer*, and the operating system empties the entire buffer when it is full. The process has to wait only if it tries to output an item before the system has emptied the buffer.

The technique can be refined by the use of two buffers rather than one; this is called *double buffering*. A process now transfers data to (or from) one buffer while the operating system empties (or fills) the other. This ensures that the process will wait only if both buffers are filled (or exhausted) before the operating system has taken action. This will happen only when the process performs a rapid burst of I/O, and in this case the problem can often be solved by the addition of yet more buffers (*multiple buffering*). Of course, no amount of buffering can help those cases in which a process demands I/O at a rate which is consistently higher than that at which the I/O devices can work. The usefulness of buffering is restricted to smoothing out peaks in I/O demand, in situations where the average demand is no greater than the I/O devices can service. In general, the higher the peaks the greater the number of buffers required to achieve the smoothing.

Specification of whether or not a stream is to be buffered may be done when it is opened; in the buffered case the user may specify how many buffers are to be used, or allow the system to supply a default value, typically two. The operating system allocates space for buffers when the stream is opened, and records their addresses in the stream descriptor.

A slightly different I/O procedure is needed to allow for buffered operation. The new procedure handles an input request by extracting the next item from the appropriate buffer and passing it directly to the calling process. Only when a buffer becomes empty does the procedure generate an IORB and signal to the device handler to supply more input. When the stream is opened the I/O procedure generates enough IORBs to fill all the buffers. The device handler operates as before, initiating a data transfer into the buffer whose location is indicated in the IORB. Similar remarks apply, *mutatis mutandis*, to output requests. In both cases the I/O procedure and the device handler together form a variation of the producer-consumer pair described in chapter 3.

The I/O procedure for buffered operations can be called from a user process by a statement of the general form

DOBUFFIO(*stream, mode, destination*)

where *stream*, *mode*, and *destination* are as described for procedure DOIO in section 6.2. The amount of information transferred will be a single item. Note that since any delays resulting from full or empty buffers are hidden in the I/O procedure, there is no need to pass a semaphore address as one of the parameters. The type of buffering, if any, the addresses of the buffers, and the semaphore to be used by the I/O procedure are all accessible from the stream descriptor list of the calling process (see figure 6.4 (b)). The first element of this information can be used to determine which I/O procedure to call to effect a transfer.

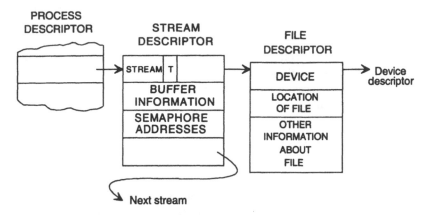

(a) File device

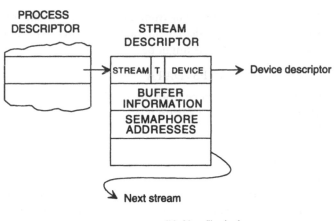

(b) Non-file device

Figure 6.4 Stream information for file and non-file devices
(T=device type)

6.5 File devices

In the foregoing discussion we have implicitly assumed that the name of a peripheral device provides sufficient information to determine the external source or destination of a given transfer. This is true of peripherals which operate sequentially, so that there is no ambiguity about the area of the external medium to (or from) which a data transfer is directed. A keyboard reader, for example, can read only the next character typed, while a printer can normally print only on the current line. In some cases it may be possible to advance the medium by a certain amount (to a new page, say), but there is no question of being able to direct a transfer to any part of the medium at will. Other devices, such as disk drives, which operate in a random access mode, provide the facility of selecting a particular area of the medium on which to effect the transfer. In these cases it is not sufficient to name the device involved; it is also necessary to specify which part of the medium is to be used to store or retrieve data.

Each data area which can exist on such media is called a *file*, and usually has an arbitrary size which is defined when it is created or updated. A device which supports files is called a *file device* or a *file structured device*. We shall say more in the next chapter about the organisation of files; for the moment we shall assume that each file has a unique name which can be used by the operating system to determine the location of the file on the appropriate medium. A directory of file names and the corresponding locations is kept by the operating system for this purpose.

When a data stream is to be directed to or from a file device, the stream has to be associated with the name of a particular file rather than with the name of the device. A typical command to do this might be

DEFINE   INPUT1   DISK3:TESTDATA

indicating that data on stream 1 is to come from the file TESTDATA, which is to be found on device DISK3. When the stream is opened the operating system looks up the file name in the directory, to find the particular location where the file is stored. This procedure, known as *opening* the file, includes various checks which will be detailed in the next chapter; because it can be a lengthy operation it is not desirable to repeat it for each data transfer. Consequently, each time a file is opened a *file descriptor* is created to hold the information which will be required for forthcoming transfers. This information includes

(1) the address of the device descriptor for the device on which the file is stored

(2) the location of the file on that device

(3) whether the file is to be written to or read from

(4) details of the file's internal organisation

A pointer to the file descriptor is placed in the appropriate stream descriptor of the process opening the file, as illustrated in figure 6.4 (a). The reader will see from a comparison of figures 6.4 (a) and 6.4 (b) that the file descriptor adds extra information to the association of streams with physical devices. The I/O procedures, which perform the association for each data transfer, can readily be modified to take this information into account when assembling an IORB.

6.6 Spooling

The preceding sections have made an implicit distinction between shareable devices, such as disk drives, which can handle successive requests from different processes, and unshareable devices, such as keyboards and printers, which can necessarily be allocated to only one process at a time. The unshareable devices are those which operate in such a way that their allocation to several processes at once would lead to an inextricable mingling of I/O transactions. As pointed out in section 6.1, the allocation of an unshareable device is made when a process opens a stream associated with it; the device is released only when the stream is closed or the process terminates. Processes which wish to use a device when it is already allocated must wait for it to be released. This implies that during periods of high demand several processes may be held up waiting for the use of scarce devices, while during other periods these same devices may be lying unused. In order to spread the load and reduce the possibility of bottlenecks some other strategy may be needed.

The solution adopted by many systems is to *spool* all I/O for heavily used devices. This means that instead of performing a transfer directly on the device associated with a stream, the I/O procedures execute the transfer on some intermediate medium, usually disk. The responsibility of moving data between the disk and the required device is vested in a separate process, called a *spooler*, which is associated with that device.

As an example, consider a system in which all printer output is spooled. Each process which opens a printer stream is allocated an anonymous file on disk, and all output on the stream is directed to this file by the I/O procedure. The file is in effect acting as a virtual printer. When the stream is closed the file is added to a queue of similar files created by other processes, all of which are waiting to be printed. The function of the printer spooler is to take files from the queue and send them to the printer. It is assumed, of course, that over a period of time the speed of the printer is adequate to handle all the output files generated. A skeletal structure for the spooler is

```
repeat indefinitely
begin wait(something to spool);
      pick file from queue;
      open file;
      repeat until end of file;
      begin DOIO(parameters for disk read);
            wait(disk request serviced);
            DOIO(parameters for printer output);
            wait(printer request serviced)
      end
end;
```

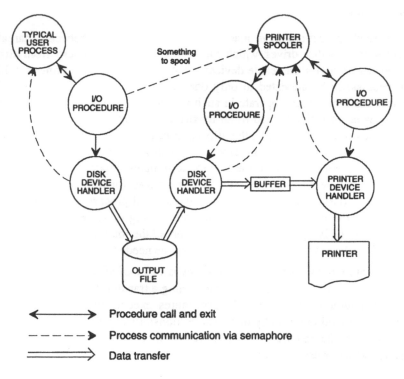

Figure 6.5 Output spooling

The reader may note the following points.

(1) The structure will in practice be modified to allow for buffering the data between disk and printer.

(2) The semaphore *something to spool* is signalled by any process which closes a printer stream (that is, completes an output file).

(3) The output queue need not be processed on a first come, first served basis; the spooler may for example favour short files over long ones.

The relationships between the spooler, the device handlers, and the processes producing the output are summarised in figure 6.5. A similar diagram, based on an analogous discussion to the above, could be drawn for an input spooler.

In summary we can say that spooling evens out the pressure of demand on heavily used peripherals. As we shall see in chapter 8, it also reduces the possibility of deadlock arising from injudicious peripheral allocation. A further advantage is that it is relatively easy to produce several copies of the same output without rerunning the job. On the debit side are the large amounts of disk space needed to hold the input and output queues, and the heavy traffic on the disk channel. Finally, spooling is of course not feasible in a real-time environment since I/O transactions are required immediately.

6.7 Conclusion

In the preceding sections we have outlined an I/O system which satisfies the objectives of character code independence, device independence, and the uniform treatment of devices. These qualities have been gained at the expense of efficiency; the I/O procedures and device handlers we presented will, because of their generalised nature, work more slowly than specialised pieces of code tailor-made for particular I/O operations or devices. However, the framework we have laid down is conceptually sound, and may be used as a basis for optimisation. The greatest gains would in practice come from replacing the code of the I/O procedures and device handlers, which is driven by information in I/O requests and device descriptors, by pieces of program specifically designed for each device and operation. This would of course blur the uniform approach we have established.

The current stage of development of the paper operating system is shown in figure 6.6.

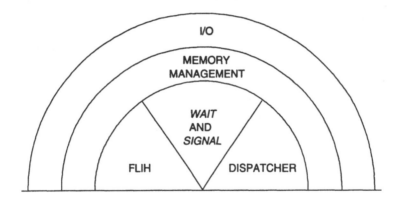

Figure 6.6 Current state of the paper operating system

7 The Filing System

7.1 Objectives

It was mentioned in chapter 2 that the facility for long-term storage is a desirable characteristic of an operating system. The motivation for long-term storage varies according to the nature of the system, but generally derives from consideration of one or more of the following benefits.

(1) On-line storage

For certain applications concerned with information retrieval (such as management information systems) it is necessary to store large quantities of data in such a way that they are always accessible. Even in a general purpose system where a large on-line database may not be essential, it is a great convenience to the user to be able to store programs or data within the computing system itself rather than on some external medium. In multi-access systems in particular it is impracticable to expect the user to manage without on-line storage, since the only I/O device available is the interactive terminal. Few users would tolerate a system in which all their programs and data had to be typed in afresh at the start of every session on the terminal. Even in batch systems, most information is stored on-line once it has been introduced to the system via relatively slow means such as input from terminals.

(2) Sharing of information

In some systems, it is desirable that users should be able to share information. For example, the users of a general purpose system may wish to use each others' programs or data, and in a transaction processing system many separate programs may use the same database. In most general purpose systems it is desirable for the installation to provide a set of library programs, such as editors, compilers, or useful procedures, which are commonly available to its users. If information is to be shared in this way then it must be stored on-line over long periods of time.

For reasons of economy long-term storage is effected on secondary media such as disks and magnetic tapes, and it is the purpose of the *filing system* to provide the means of organising and accessing the data in a way convenient to the user. The way this is done will naturally depend on the kind of data and the uses to which it is to be put; the filing system for a transaction processing system can be expected to be quite different from that for a process control system. In this chapter we shall keep to the spirit of the book in confining ourselves to general purpose systems, in which the filing systems are generally disk based; the reader who is interested in other areas is referred to the extensive literature elsewhere (for example QIC, Inc.; ISO, 1988; Folk *et al.*, 1987).

The user of a general purpose system arranges data in *files* of arbitrary size. Each file is thus a collection of data which is regarded as an entity by the user; it may be a program, a set of procedures, or the results of an experiment. The file is the logical unit which is stored and manipulated by the filing system. The medium on which files are stored is usually divided into *blocks* of fixed length (typically 512 to 4096 bytes), and the filing system must allocate the appropriate number of blocks to each file.

In order to be useful the filing system must

(1) allow creation and deletion of files

(2) allow access to files for reading or writing

(3) perform automatic management of secondary memory space. The exact whereabouts of files in secondary memory should be of no concern to the user

(4) allow reference to files by symbolic name. Since the user does not know, nor wish to know, the physical location of the files, it should be necessary only to quote their names in order to refer to them

(5) protect files against system failure. Users will be reluctant to commit themselves to the system unless convinced of its integrity

(6) allow the sharing of files among co-operating users but protect files against access by unauthorised users

In the following sections we examine how these objectives can be achieved.

7.2 File directories

The basic problem in accessing a file is to map a symbolic file name to a physical location in secondary memory. The mapping is achieved by means of a *file directory*, or *catalogue*, which is basically a table containing information about the locations of named files. Since the directory is the mechanism through which the file is accessed, it is natural to include in it some means of protection against unauthorised access. We shall discuss this further in the next section; for the present we observe that an immediate measure of security can be afforded by dividing the directory into two levels as shown in figure 7.1. At the upper level a *master file directory* (MFD) contains for each user in the system a pointer to a *user file directory* (UFD) for that user; at the lower level each UFD contains the names and locations of a single user's files. Since a UFD can be accessed only via the MFD, the privacy of a user's files can be assured by a simple identity check at the MFD level. Moreover, it is possible for different users to use the same name for a file without confusion, since the *full name* of a file can be regarded as the concatenation of the user name (or number) with the *individual name* of the file. For example, the individual name of the file shown in figure 7.1 is PROG, and its full name is FRED/PROG (the actual separator character is a matter of syntax only; it is not actually stored within the filing system). In practice it is not always necessary to specify the full name of a file, since the filing system can use the identity of the person requesting access as the default value for the first component. Only when a user requests access to another user's file is it necessary to quote the name in full.

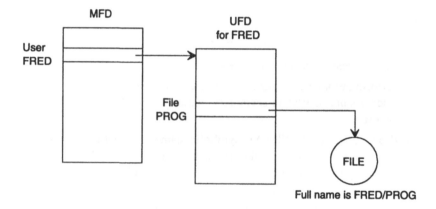

Figure 7.1 Two-level directory structure

The information in each UFD generally includes the following.

(1) The file name.

(2) The physical location of the file in secondary memory. The form of this entry will depend on the way in which the file is stored (see section 7.4).

(3) The file type (character, binary relocatable, binary executable, library, etc.). This information is kept largely for user convenience, and also for the convenience of system components and programs, such as loaders or editors, which may be used to operate on the file. For example, a print spooler could use the file type to prevent attempts to print the contents of an executable program file; such an attempt is likely to be the result of a mistake on the part of a user. So far as the filing system is concerned each file is simply a string of bytes (or even bits).

(4) Access control information (for example 'read only'; see section 7.3).

(5) Administrative information (time of last update or time last copy taken). This information, besides being of interest to the user, is necessary to provide data for the system activities of preserving duplicate copies as insurance against hardware failure (see section 7.5).

Some systems adopt the two-level directory structure described above. Many others (such as MS-DOS, UNIX and VMS) extend the concept to a multi-level structure, in which directory entries may be pointers to either files or other directories (see figure 7.2). A multi-level structure is useful in situations where the stored data has a tree-like classification, or where the users are grouped in hierarchies such as individuals within project teams within departments. In the latter case a hierarchical protection mechanism can be applied by making increasingly stringent checks as one progresses further down the tree. As in the two-level system, conflicting file names can be resolved by regarding the full name of the file as the concatenation of its individual name with the names of the directories on its access path. In some systems, the master file directory is referred to as the *root directory*.

The disadvantage of a multi-level system lies in the length of the path to any particular file and the number of disk accesses which must be made to follow the path through the various directories. This can be alleviated to some

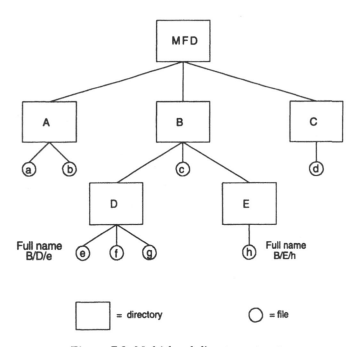

Figure 7.2 Multi-level directory structure

extent by making use of the tendency of successive file accesses to be directed to files in the same directory. Once a route has been established through the tree structure to a particular directory then this directory can be designated the current directory and subsequent file references need only quote the individual file name. A change of current directory is made by quoting the file name in full. This technique is used in UNIX (Ritchie and Thompson, 1974; Bach, 1986) and MS-DOS (Duncan, 1988), among many others.

Another efficiency consideration is the way is which information is organised within each directory. The simplest way is to divide the directory into fixed size slots, each of which contains the information about a single file. Whenever a file is created, the next empty slot is used; when a file is deleted, the slot is marked free. This results in a directory which may be a good deal bigger than necessary, particularly if it has held a larger number of entries at some time in the past. A further problem is the trade-off between the maximum length of filename and the resulting wasted space in many directory entries.

When a file is to be looked up in the directory, a simple linear scan is often employed; large directories naturally do not perform well. Various solutions have been employed to mitigate this problem; one is the use of tree structures to maintain the directory in a sorted order (see Duncan, 1990, for an example of a system using these).

7.3 Sharing and security

The problem of the security of files arises directly from the desire to share them. In a non-sharing environment, where the only person allowed to access a file is the owner, security can be achieved by making an identity check in the MFD. When files are to be shared, however, a means is required of specifying which users are to be allowed access to the owner's files, and which are not. Moreover it is convenient for the owner to be able to specify *what kind* of access is to be permitted; it may be desirable that some colleagues should be able to update the files, others only to read them, and others merely to execute their contents as programs or sequences of system commands. We summarise this by saying that the owner must be able to specify what *access privileges* other users may have.

A particularly simple way of doing this is to associate with each file a set of access privileges (or *protection mask*) applicable to various classes of user. The user classes might be

(1) the owner (O)

(2) group members or partners (G)

(3) others, or the 'rest of the world' (W)

and typical access privileges are

(1) read access (R)

(2) write access (W)

(3) execute access (E)

(4) delete access (D)

A typical protection mask assigned by the owner when creating the file might be

O:RWED,G:RW,W:R

meaning that the owner can do anything, partners can read and write, and anyone else can only read. The file protection mask resides in the owner's UFD as part of the entry for that particular file. Note that in some cases it may be sensible for owners to grant themselves limited access in order to protect them from their own mistakes (for example, removing delete access in order to avoid accidental deletion of an important file). The filing system must of course always allow owners to change the protection masks on all files which belong to them.

An implication of this method is that there must be division of the user population into *groups* for the purpose of determining access to files. This is often done by structuring the identification by which the user is known to the system (the *user identification code* or *UIC*) so that one component indicates the group to which the user belongs, and the other provides the individual user identity. This technique is clearly inadequate when different but overlapping partnerships are required for different files; some systems (including later versions of UNIX) tackle this problem by allowing a user to belong to more than one group.

A more general technique, which overcomes the hierarchical limitations of user grouping, is to use *access control lists*; VMS and Windows NT are examples of systems which use this approach.

An access control list (or ACL) may be attached to a file or to a directory, and provides complete information about users allowed to access the specified object. Sometimes it is used in combination with the simpler methods outlined earlier.

An ACL consists of one or more *access control entries* (or ACEs), each of which specifies the kind of access allowed to a specified user or group of users. The ordering of the list is important, since when access is checked the ACL is searched from its beginning; a user may appear implicitly more than once in the same ACL, and generally it is the first entry matching that user which is used to determine access.

Each access control entry consists of the following.

(1) A specification of a user or group of users to which this ACE applies. This could be a user name, a group name, or even the name of some access token which must be held by the user in order to match the entry; normally such a token would be granted by the system manager.

(2) A definition of the access privileges accorded by this ACE; these follow the normal form (for example, RWED).

(3) Options associated with the ACE; for example, in the case of an ACE attached to a directory, whether the ACE should be propagated to any files created in that directory.

Generally, if users attempt access to a file which has an ACL attached, and they do not appear anywhere in the list, the normal protection mask is then used to make the final decision about the kind of access (if any) to be allowed. It is often useful to attach a 'match-all' entry to the tail of the ACL, thus ensuring that the normal protection mask is never consulted.

The main problem with ACLs is that they often take up a large amount of space, and slow down access to files; unless the increased flexibility is essential then this method should probably not be used.

Another technique, first used in MULTICS (Organick, 1972) is for an owner to allow other users to create *links* in their UFDs to entries within his or

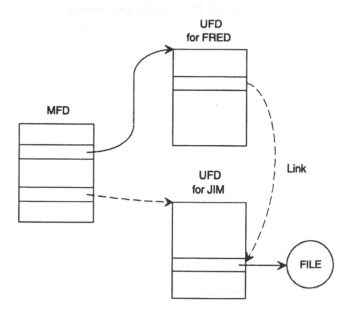

Figure 7.3 Links between UFDs

her own UFD. Figure 7.3 shows a user FRED who has a link to a file entry in the UFD belonging to another user JIM. The link allows FRED to access the corresponding file belonging to JIM. JIM's UFD will contain a list of all users whom he allows to make such links. The great disadvantage of this method is that when a file is deleted all links to it must also be deleted, which means that the system must have a way of finding where all the links are.

A similar system is used in UNIX under the name of a *hard link*; here the link is effectively directly to the file rather than to a UFD entry, and this link is indistinguishable from the original UFD entry. A count is maintained of the number of links to a file, and the file is deleted only when the count drops to zero. Access to the file is controlled by permissions attached to each file rather than to each UFD entry. Hard links are useful, but require write access to the directory in which the file appears, and they cannot operate between directories and files residing on separate logical disks (because a link to a file may exist on a disk that is not available when that file is deleted). Later versions of UNIX thus supplement hard links with *symbolic links*. These are special directory entries that simply contain, as a target, the name of the file to which the link refers; there is no backward linkage, so the worst that can happen is that the link can point to a file that no longer exists. In such a case, a simple error message is sufficient since there is no danger to the integrity of the structures making up the filing system.

Summarising, the techniques just described offer various solutions to the problem of sharing and security. In general the more flexible the method adopted the greater the space overhead in the UFDs and the longer the time to perform an access.

7.4 Secondary memory organisation

As mentioned in section 7.1 file storage is generally allocated in blocks, and since file sizes are variable, some kind of dynamic storage technique is required for both files and free space. There are several ways of organising the blocks within a file, four of which we describe next. We assume that the blocks on a disk are numbered in some way, probably from one up to the total number of blocks on the disk (there may also be a block zero, but generally this is used in some special way by hardware or for system initialisation).

Note that the descriptions given below are presented in a basic form; in practice, there are usually modifications and embellishments. One notable addition can be the inclusion of redundant information, used when reconstructing a damaged file system (see Duncan, 1990, for a good example of this).

(1) Contiguous files

All of the blocks in the file are adjacent (that is, they have consecutive numbers). The UFD entry for the file points to the first block, and also contains the length of the file. There is little in the way of storage overhead; the whole of each block is used to hold user data.

This is the simplest method of organisation; it is sometimes used on small single-user systems and personal computers. It is easy to implement, but suffers from *fragmentation*; as files are created and deleted, the free space becomes broken up into small pieces, none of which may be large enough by itself to hold anything but the smallest file. It is thus necessary to perform regular *compaction*, which moves files around in order to merge the free space into one or more usable areas. Compaction usually has to take place on a quiescent file system, which precludes the use of this technique by all except single-user systems. It is difficult to add or delete blocks in the middle of a file, since this implies the movement of all following data. There are also problems linked to the efficient allocation of space on occasions when it is not known, at the time the first block is allocated, what the final size of a file will be.

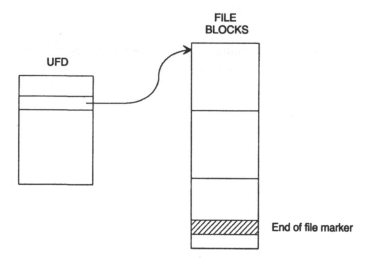

Figure 7.4 Contiguous file blocks

Despite these problems, contiguous files do have some advantages. First, they present an extremely resilient way of organising data; damage to a single block results in only localised loss of data. In addition, any block may be accessed at random by use of simple arithmetic, making contiguous files a good choice for applications such as databases where some kind of additional internal structure may be needed. Because of this, contiguous files are often included as an alternative method in other filing systems, to be used when specially requested.

(2) Block linkage

A few bytes in each block of the file are used as a pointer to the next block (see figure 7.5). The last block contains a null pointer (typically zero). The UFD entry for the file points to the first block in the chain. The space overhead involved is the space occupied by these few bytes (typically four) per block for each file.

A disadvantage of this method of chaining is the large number of disk accesses which are needed to find the end of the file. This can be particularly inconvenient if the file is to be deleted and the space occupied returned to a free list; the alterations to pointers which are required to return the space rely on a knowledge of the position of the end of the file. For this reason the UFD entry is often extended to point to the last block in the file as well as to the first.

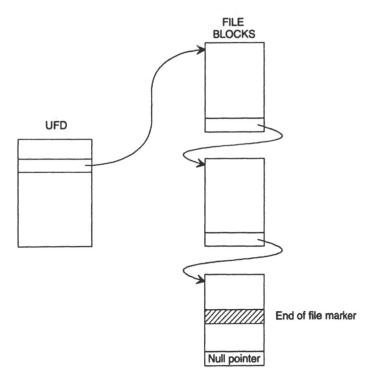

Figure 7.5 Linked file blocks

The reader will note that access to the file is necessarily sequential since all blocks can be accessed only by passing down the chain. This method of chaining is therefore best suited to situations in which the files are processed sequentially. In these cases the overhead in accessing the file is only that of reading the successive blocks.

The resilience of this method is low. Damage to one block (and the link contained within it) can result in creeping damage to the whole file system, as unwanted cross-linkage proliferates. Storage of redundant reverse links, while an additional overhead, can assist greatly in reducing this problem.

(3) File map

For this method of file linkage, the state of the disk is recorded in a *file map* or *file allocation table* in which each disk block is represented by a single map entry. The UFD entry for a file points to the location in the file map which represents the first block in the file. This location in turn points to the location in the map which represents the next block in the file, and so on (see figure 7.6). The last block in the file is represented by a null pointer, again typically zero. Thus the file shown in figure 7.6 occupies blocks 3, 6, 4 and 8 of the disk. The space overhead of the method depends on the size of a map entry; on small disks (such as floppy disks on personal computers) it can be as little as 12 bits, while on larger systems it may be 32 bits. Map entries may also

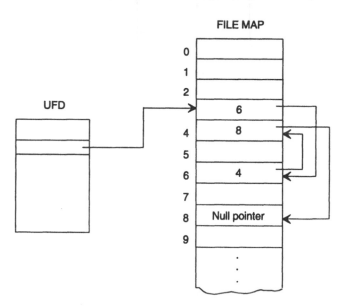

Figure 7.6 File map

contain additional redundant information such as a unique file identification number; this can be useful when recovering files after a system failure.

As with the block linkage method, access to the file is necessarily sequential. As an aid to extending and deleting a file the UFD entry may contain a pointer to the location in the file map which represents the last block in the file.

Since the file map is generally too large to be held in main memory it must be stored on disk itself and brought into memory one block at a time as required. This means that to read a file of N blocks may require an extra N disk accesses to read the appropriate parts of the file map. The overhead will be less than this only if some of the locations representing successive blocks of the file happen to lie in the same block of the file map. For this reason it is clearly advantageous to keep the space occupied by each file as nearly contiguous as possible, rather than allowing the file to be spread over the entire disk.

Damage to the file map is likely to cause serious data loss. This can be eliminated by storing two or more copies of the map. Naturally, the copies should be kept in different areas of the disk, or a hardware failure is likely to damage all of the copies (as indeed it can in MS-DOS, where all of the maps are stored in a contiguous area).

(4) Index blocks

The linkage pointers for each file are stored in a separate *index block* on disk. If the file is large then several index blocks may be needed, each one chained to the next (see figure 7.7). The UFD entry for the file points to the first index block in the chain. Since the last index block for a file is unlikely to be fully used the average space overhead is slightly more than one index block entry (typically, four bytes) per block for each file. The overhead for small files is proportionately greater than for large ones. This problem is tackled in UNIX by storing a small primary index area effectively as part of the directory entry (actually, in a small area, called an *i-node*, pointed to by the directory entry). Files with only a few blocks can be described completely by the contents of the i-node; larger files use a normal index block pointed to by the i-node.

The great advantage of index blocks is that the file need not be accessed sequentially; any block may be accessed at random simply by specifying the name of the file and an offset in the index block. This method of file storage therefore lends itself to situations in which files possess an internal structure and in which the individual components are to be accessed separately.

The time overhead in accessing the file is small; the first access requires the index block to be read, but subsequent accesses carry no overhead unless different index blocks are needed. However, the addition or deletion of blocks

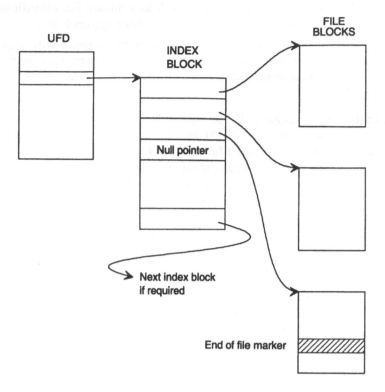

Figure 7.7 Use of index blocks

in the middle of the file implies a rearrangement of pointers in the index blocks. This can be a lengthy operation and means that this method of storage is unsuitable for files which change frequently.

A variation of this technique (used on VMS) stores a series of *extent descriptors* in the equivalent of an index block. Each extent descriptor consists of a disk block number and a length in blocks; this uses much less space so long as the disk is not heavily fragmented.

Damage to index blocks results in severe data loss. This is often mitigated by storing multiple copies of the index blocks in different areas of the disk; this is a substantial overhead but it provides a good solution.

We remark in passing that in each of the above methods the end of each file can be denoted by a special marker at the appropriate place in the last block. This can be done for any type of file for which a unique marker can be defined which cannot be interpreted as data. For example, the end of file marker for character files could be a bit pattern which does not represent any known character; unfortunately, with the advent of extended character sets on many systems, such a bit pattern may not always exist. No such marker can be defined for binary files since all bit patterns form valid data. It is thus necessary to record the length of a file as an extra component in its UFD entry. (This is probably a good idea in any case, since it can give an extra check against corruption of a file and is also an item of information frequently required by users.)

As a final observation on file block linkage we remark that a system may allow several forms of linkage, particularly where some files are likely to be accessed sequentially, and others non-sequentially. The type of linkage required may be specified by the user when a file is created, with a suitable default being supplied by the system.

An equally important aspect of secondary memory organisation is the management of free space. One method is to regard free blocks as constituting a file in their own right, and to link them by one of the techniques described above. In the case of contiguous files, each series of consecutive blocks forms a separate 'free' file. If the index block technique is used then all operations on a free chain (that is, allocating and returning free blocks) must take place at its tail since operations at the head would involve the rearrangement of a large number of pointers. If the block linkage or file map technique is used the operations may take place at either end of the chain. The index block technique has the further disadvantage that when N blocks are allocated or returned then N pointers must be deleted from or inserted in the last index block. By contrast only two pointers need changing when the other two techniques are used, no matter how many blocks are allocated or returned. (For example, when blocks are returned to the end of the free chain the two pointers which need changing are one from the last block of the old chain to the first block of the addition, and one from the system directory to the end of the new chain.)

A different method of recording free space is to use a *bit map*, which is an area of memory in which each bit represents a disk block. If a block is free the corresponding bit is set to zero; if the block is being used the bit is set to one. In order to find N free blocks it is necessary only to search the bit map for the first N zero bits, and then perform a simple calculation to obtain the corresponding block addresses.

In some situations the bit map may be too large to be held conveniently in main memory. In these cases the map can be stored in secondary memory, with only a section of it in main memory. This section can be used for all allocations, and when it is full (that is, all bits are one) it can be swapped for another section. The return of free space involves retrieving that section of the map corresponding to the returned blocks, and setting the appropriate bits to zero. This may result in heavy traffic of the bit map, but this can be reduced by keeping a list of all returned blocks and using it to update the map each time a new section of it comes into main memory. This technique must be used with care, so that in the event of a disk crash the state of the bit map remains consistent with the space allocated.

The choice of block size is generally made by the hardware designer (although there are some systems where the user may make a separate choice for each file). The system designer may choose an effective block size which is a multiple of the hardware block size, and hide the true block size inside the device handler for the disk in question. The actual choice is made according to the following criteria.

(1) The waste of space due to some blocks not being completely filled. This will increase as the block size increases.

(2) The waste of space due to chain pointers. The smaller the blocks, the more pointers are required.

(3) The unit in which the storage device transfers data to main memory. The block size should be a multiple of this unit so as to fully utilise each data transfer.

(4) The amount of memory needed for each read or write operation on a file. Depending on the method of disk organisation, space may have to be found in memory for the current index block or the current file map block, as well as for the block being read or written.

Typical block sizes are 512 to 4096 bytes.

Space allocation strategies can range from the straightforward (use the first block on the free chain or the first block in the bit map) to the sophisticated (use the block which will minimise the amount of disk head movement when reading the file). This latter technique is often implemented by holding multiple lists of free blocks, one for each area of a disk (an area being all those blocks grouped in such a way as to require no head movement to move between them). The overhead of seek time in reading a file whose blocks are scattered all over the disk can in fact be quite large and can lead to saturation of the disk channel. It can be reduced by the strategy outlined above, or by periodically going through the file structure concatenating files as much as possible. This latter technique can be built into the back-up procedures described in the next section.

7.5 File system integrity

Since the content of files may represent many months' work, or may consist of irreplaceable data, it is essential that a filing system provides adequate mechanisms for back-up and recovery in the not unlikely event of hardware or software failure. This means that the system must maintain duplicate copies of all files so that they can be restored after any unfortunate occurrence.

There are two principal ways of making copies of files, the first and simpler of which is known as the *periodic* (or *massive*) dump. At fixed intervals of time the contents of the entire file store are dumped onto some medium, usually magnetic tape, and in the event of failure all files can be recreated in the state they were in when the last dump was taken. Single files which are inadvertently deleted may be retrieved at the expense of scanning the entire dump tape. The disadvantages of the periodic dump are as follows

(1) The file system may have to be placed out of use during the period of the dump. The alternative is not to dump any files which are open for writing.

(2) The dump usually takes a long time (20 minutes to 2 hours per disk, depending on the size of the system and the speed of the tape drives). This means that the dump cannot be performed very often, and so a retrieved file may well be out of date.

The second and more sophisticated technique is the *incremental dump* (Fraser, 1969). This is normally used in conjunction with a (less frequent) periodic dump. With this technique a dump is made only of that information which has been changed since the previous dump was taken. This means that only files which have been created or altered, and directory entries which have been modified, will be dumped on each occasion. The amount of such information will normally be small, and so the dump can be made at frequent intervals. In order to determine which files are to be dumped a flag in the directory entry of each file is set whenever the file is altered, and cleared when it is dumped. So that the dumping process does not have to examine all directory entries, a global flag in each UFD can be used to indicate whether any individual flags within the UFD are set. Since the dumping process will skip all files whose flags are not set, which includes all files which are currently being updated, it can run in parallel with normal work. It is even possible, as first implemented in MULTICS, for the dumper to be a low priority process which is always present in the machine and which continually searches directories looking for updated information.

The disadvantages of the incremental dump lie in the large quantities of data which are generated and in the complexity of the recovery procedure. After a failure information must be reconstructed from the sequence of events recorded on the dump tapes. The tapes are mounted in inverse chronological order, and the filing system is restored back to the time that the last periodic dump was taken. (Periodic dumps will be made at rare intervals, typically once a week.) During this procedure the reloading process picks out from the dump tapes only those files that it has not already restored, so that recent files are not superseded by earlier versions. Finally the last periodic dump tape is used to complete the recovery operation. This method of procedure is superior to starting with the periodic dump tape and working forwards, since no redundant information is restored.

Some systems, such as VMS and EMAS (Rees, 1975; Wight, 1975), record a *journal* or *directory* of the files being backed up. Clearly this should reside on a different disk, or be separately backed up in some other way. This information provides details of exactly where the latest copy of each file resides, and opens the way to more automated means of recovery (a useful point, since recovery usually needs to take place in a hurry and at a time when operators may be more than usually agitated and liable to make mistakes). Systems such as EMAS also make the actual back-up mechanism virtually automatic, requiring the operator to do no more than specify the type of back-up (periodic or incremental) and then load tapes as requested, all tape alloc-ation being performed by the system; again this reduces the chances of an error which may be discovered only when it is too late.

It is worth noting that whatever method of dumping is used the recovery of the system affords a good opportunity to compact files into contiguous blocks. This reduces file access overheads at the possible expense of slightly lengthen-ing the recovery procedure.

7.6 Opening and closing files

We remarked in the last chapter that when an I/O stream is associated with a file the operating system must look up the device and location where the file is stored. This procedure is known as *opening* the file; the inverse procedure of *closing* the file is performed either explicitly when all I/O to the file has been completed or implicitly when the process using the file terminates.

To implement these operations, we require within the operating system two procedures of the form

> *open(filename, mode)*
> *close(filename)*

where *filename* is the name of the file to be opened or closed, and *mode* is the type of access required (for example read, write or create). The operations performed by *open* are as follows.

(1) Look up the directory entry for the file.

(2) Check that the requesting process was instigated by a user with the requisite privileges for access in the specified mode.

(3) Perform checks to ensure that if the file is already open for reading (possibly by another process) it cannot now be opened for writing, and

that if it is already open for writing it cannot now be opened at all. These checks will be described in a moment.

(4) Ascertain the device and location where the file is stored. If the file is to be newly created then the location is specified by the space allocation routine.

(5) Create a *file descriptor* which contains all information about the file relevant to forthcoming data transfers. The file descriptor, as mentioned in section 6.5, is used by I/O procedures as a source of information for constructing I/O requests, thus avoiding the necessity of going through the open procedure for each data transfer involving the file.

The information required in the file descriptor includes

(1) the file name

(2) the address of the device descriptor of the device on which the file is stored

(3) the location of the first block in the file

(4) the location of the next block to be read or written (assuming that access is sequential)

(5) the mode of access

The file descriptor is pointed to from the appropriate stream descriptor of the process which has opened the file, as shown in figure 6.4(a).

The read/write interlocks referred to in part (3) of the description of *open* may be implemented by including two extra items in the directory entry of each file. The first is a 'write bit' which is set whenever the file is opened for writing; the second is a 'use count' of the number of processes which currently have the file open for reading. A process may open a file for reading only if the write bit is zero, and may open it for writing only if the write bit and the use count are both zero. Unfortunately there is a problem with this technique in that several processes might simultaneously wish to open or close the same file, thus making simultaneous changes to the directory entry. This can be overcome by writing the *open* and *close* procedures as critical sections, each enclosed by the same mutual exclusion semaphore, but this has the serious disadvantage that if a process is interrupted while opening or closing a file then these operations are unavailable to all other processes.

An alternative technique is to form a list of the file descriptors of all files which are open on each particular device. This list can be pointed to from the device descriptor of the device concerned. When a file is to be opened the *open* procedure inspects the list to see whether any file descriptors already exist for the file, and if so what mode of access they indicate. The procedure refuses to open the file unless the read/write constraints are satisfied. A mutual exclusion semaphore can be used to protect the list from simultaneous access by processes which wish to open or close the same file at the same time. The disadvantage of this technique lies in the time required to inspect the list, which in a large multi-access system might easily contain several hundred descriptors. This time is particularly critical since the list can be inspected by only one process at a time, and if the process is interrupted then the list becomes inaccessible to other processes.

A partial solution to these problems is to divide each file descriptor into two separate structures: a *central file descriptor* for each open file and a *local file descriptor* for each process using a file. A local file descriptor is created each time a process opens a file, and all the local file descriptors for a particular file point to the single central file descriptor for that file. The central file descriptors are linked to the appropriate device descriptor (see figure 7.7). A central file descriptor contains information which is the same for any process using the file, namely

(1) the file name

(2) the address of the device descriptor of the device on which the file is stored

(3) the location of the first block in the file

(4) the use count for the file

(5) the write bit for the file

A local file descriptor contains information which is particular to the process using the file, namely

(1) the location of the next block to be read or written

(2) the mode of access

plus a pointer to the central file descriptor for the file. The introduction of central file descriptors eliminates the storage of duplicate information in separate descriptors and reduces the length of the descriptor list for each device. It also reduces the amount of work that the *open* and *close* procedures have to do in searching the descriptor list. More significantly, it allows mutual exclusion to be applied to each descriptor separately rather than to the list as a whole, and thus it avoids the bottleneck dangers mentioned earlier. The mutual exclusion semaphore can be held in the central file descriptor for each file.

A variation of this technique (Courtois *et al.*, 1971) is to replace the write bit in the central file descriptor by another semaphore w. The *open* and *close* procedures are then written to include the following pieces of code.

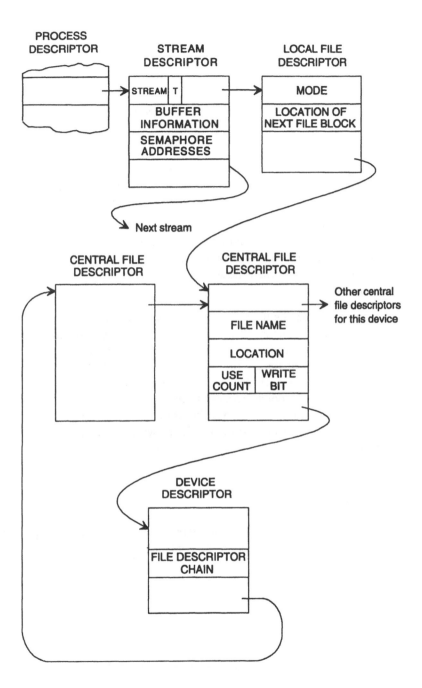

Figure 7.8 Local and central file descriptors

Open	*Close*
if *mode* = read **then**	**if** *mode* = read **then**
begin *wait(mutex)*;	**begin** *wait(mutex)*;
usecount : = *usecount* + 1;	*usecount* : = *usecount* - 1;
if *usecount* = 1 **then**	**if** *usecount* = 0 **then**
wait(w);	*signal(w)*;
signal(mutex)	*signal(mutex)*
end	**end**
else *wait(w)*;	**else** *signal(w)*;

In this variation those access requests which are refused are implicitly queued on the semaphore *w*, while in the original version the system designer retains the freedom to queue requests or not, according to the application.

The operation of the *close* procedure is relatively simple. It consists of deleting the local file descriptor and decrementing the use count in the central file descriptor. If the use count is zero the central file descriptor is also deleted and the directory updated where necessary (if, for example, the file has just been created).

Deletion of a file may be treated as a call of *open* with an appropriate *mode* parameter. However this has the disadvantage that if the file is already open, as will often be the case with library files, the delete request will be refused. This makes the replacement of library files somewhat awkward. A way round this problem is to include in each central file descriptor a 'delete pending bit' which is set whenever a delete request is made on an open file. The *close* procedure checks this bit: if it is set and the use count falls to zero the file can be deleted. Deletion is hastened if *open* refuses access to a file whose delete pending bit is set.

7.7 Conclusion

In this chapter we have discussed various aspects of filing systems for general purpose applications. The next step in the construction of our paper operating system is the adoption of a particular system based on the techniques we have described. This will give us another layer of our 'onion', consisting of code for implementing particular security and integrity mechanisms, for administering free space, and for opening and closing files. The additional permanent data structures are the file directories and whatever structure is used to record space allocation. Temporary data structures which exist only while a file is open are the local and central file descriptors. The current state of the system is shown in figure 7.9.

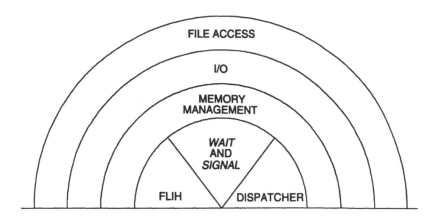

Figure 7.9 Current state of the paper operating system

8 Resource Allocation and Scheduling

Up to this point in the development of our paper operating system we have assumed that all processes have the resources they need. It is now time to consider how processes acquire their resources, and how a limited set of resources can be effectively shared among several processes. Our discussion of resource allocation will also include scheduling since the two functions are closely related: decisions on process priority can be dependent on where resources are committed, and the introduction of new processes into the system is clearly influenced by the amount of spare resource capacity. In fact scheduling, being concerned with the allocation of central processors, can be regarded as a subtopic of resource allocation as a whole.

8.1 General observations

In an environment in which resources were unlimited a 'grab it when you need it' method of acquisition would be perfectly acceptable. Unfortunately, it is rarely feasible to provide resources to satisfy the concurrent demands of all processes in the system, and so techniques must be devised to share a limited set of resources among a number of competing processes. The objectives of these techniques are to

(1) mutually exclude processes from unshareable resources

(2) prevent deadlock (see section 3.2) arising in respect of resource requests

(3) ensure a high level of resource utilisation

(4) allow all processes an opportunity to acquire the resources they need within a 'reasonable' time

The reader will see that these objectives are not necessarily mutually consistent. In particular, the user satisfaction implied by objective (4) can generally be gained only by compromising objective (3). This is because the higher the level of resource utilisation the longer will be the average wait before a resource request can be granted. The trade-off between user satisfaction and resource utilisation is one of the criteria by which resource allocation and scheduling policies can be evaluated. In a real-time system with a guaranteed response time one would expect the trade-off to be in favour of the user; in a batch system it might be in favour of high utilisation. This can create a difficult managerial problem in a system which attempts to provide both batch and interactive service.

It is useful to discuss resource allocation under two headings: the *mechanisms* and the *policies*. By *mechanisms* we mean the nuts and bolts aspect of how allocation is made. This includes such things as data structures for describing the state of resources, techniques for ensuring the exclusive use of unshareable resources, and means for queueing resource requests which cannot be granted immediately. The *policies* govern the ways in which the mechanisms are applied. They are concerned with the wisdom of granting requests even when the appropriate resources are available. This involves the questions of deadlock and system balance: an unwise allocation may lead to a situation in which some processes cannot proceed or in which the system is overloaded with respect to one particular class of resource. It is at this latter point that resource allocation becomes linked with scheduling, since the likelihood of overload can be reduced by judicious scheduling decisions regarding process priority and the introduction of new processes into the system. We shall discuss both mechanisms and policies in the following sections.

8.2 Allocation mechanisms

From the observations above it should be apparent that any element of a computing system which is in limited supply, and which has to be shared, can be regarded as a resource. In fact resources generally fall into one of the categories mentioned next. We shall review the allocation mechanisms for each category, giving consideration to what part of the system makes the allocation, the data structures used to describe the resources, and the means by which processes are queued while awaiting allocation.

(1) Central processors

We have already discussed in chapter 4 how a central processor is allocated by the dispatcher to the first non-running process in the processor queue. The data describing a central processor can be held in a processor descriptor which is similar to the device descriptor used for data relating to a peripheral (see chapter 6). The processor descriptor might typically contain

   (a) the processor identification

   (b) the current status – whether in user or supervisor mode

   (c) a pointer to the process descriptor of the current process

The processor descriptors can be contained within the central table, or can be pointed to from it.

In a configuration in which processors are dissimilar, the processor descriptors can be extended to hold an indication of the individual processor characteristics (for example, whether it has floating point hardware). In this case each processor might be best suited to running a particular kind of process, and so might have its own processor queue pointed to from its descriptor. The processor queues are then analogous to the device request queues for peripherals. The assignment of processes to different processor queues is a subject still largely unexplored, and we shall not deal further with it here.

(2) Memory

In chapter 5 we saw how memory can be allocated by the memory management layer of the operating system in both the paged and non-paged cases. The data structures describing the state of memory are the page tables, segment tables, or free block lists, depending on the memory management architecture involved. A process waiting for the transfer of a new page or segment from secondary memory is made unrunnable, with the status bits in its process descriptor indicating the reason. Page and segment requests are queued as I/O request blocks by the memory management system, and serviced by the device handler for the appropriate secondary memory device.

(3) Peripherals

We described in chapter 6 how, in systems with stream based I/O, an unshareable peripheral is allocated to a process when the corresponding stream is opened. In systems which do not use streams a peripheral may be allocated after a direct request to the operating system. In both cases the allocation mechanism is the same. The data structure describing a peripheral is its device descriptor, and processes awaiting allocation of a peripheral can be queued on a semaphore which is included in the descriptor. Mutual exclusion in the use of the peripheral is ensured by initialising the semaphore value to one.

(4) Backing store

Backing store which is used in the implementation of virtual memory is allocated by the memory management system, and that used as file space is allocated by the filing system. Some operating systems, notably MULTICS (Organick, 1972) and EMAS (Rees, 1975), make no distinction between files and segments, so that the file store becomes part of the virtual memory and the filing system is responsible for all allocations. The data structure used for allocation is some kind of free block list or bit map as described in section 7.4.

Requests for file space are refused only when an individual user has exceeded his or her quota, or when all backing store is full. In neither case is it sensible to queue requests; the former situation can be resolved only by the user's own action, and the latter situation cannot be guaranteed to change within any small space of time.

(5) *Files*

An individual file may be regarded as a resource in the sense that several processes may wish to share it. So long as all processes operate in a 'read only' mode the resource is shareable; if one process wishes to write to the file then the resource is unshareable.

Allocation of a file to a process is made by the filing system when the file is opened, and write interlocks are achieved by the methods described in section 7.6. The data structures describing files are of course the file directories.

Batch systems do not usually queue file requests since simultaneous (non-read) requests are usually indicative of user error. However, in transaction processing or process control it may well be sensible to establish access queues within the filing system. These queues may be associated with semaphores as discussed in section 7.6.

It is apparent from the above review that allocation mechanisms are implemented at various levels of the operating system, each mechanism being found at the level appropriate to the resource being allocated. We shall see, however, that the policies for using the mechanisms must be global to the entire system.

8.3 Deadlock

The first resource allocation policies we consider are concerned with the problem of deadlock, which was described in section 3.2.

If resources are allocated to processes solely on the basis of their availability then deadlock may easily occur. In its simplest form deadlock will happen in the following circumstances: process *A* is granted resource *X* and then requests resource *Y*; process *B* is granted resource *Y* and then requests resource *X*. If both resources are unshareable and neither process will release the resource it holds then deadlock ensues. In general the necessary and sufficient conditions for deadlock (Coffman *et al.*, 1971; Minoura, 1982) are as follows.

(1) The resources involved are unshareable.

(2) Processes hold the resources they have already been allocated while waiting for new ones.

(3) Resources cannot be pre-empted while being used.

(4) A circular chain of processes exists such that each process holds resources which are currently being requested by the next process in the chain.

The problem of deadlock may be solved by adopting one of the following strategies.

(1) Prevent deadlock by ensuring at all times that at least one of the four conditions above does not hold.

(2) Detect deadlock when it occurs and then try to recover.

(3) Avoid deadlock by suitable anticipatory action.

We consider each of these strategies in turn.

(1) Deadlock prevention

To prevent deadlock, at least one of the four necessary conditions above must be denied.

Condition (1) is difficult to deny since some resources (for example a printer or a writeable file) are by nature unshareable. However, the use of spooling (see section 6.6) can remove the deadlock potential of unshareable peripherals.

Condition (2) can be denied by stipulating that processes request all their resources at once and that they cannot proceed until all the requests are granted. This has the disadvantage that resources which are used only for a short time are nevertheless allocated and therefore inaccessible for long periods. It is, however, easy to implement, and may prove more economical in the long run than some more complex algorithm.

Condition (3) is easily denied by imposing the rule that if a process is refused a resource request then it must release all resources that it currently holds, and if necessary request them again together with the additional resources. Unfortunately this Draconian strategy can be rather inconvenient in practice, since pre-empting a printer (say) would result in the interleaving of output from several jobs. Furthermore, even if a resource is conveniently pre-emptible, the overhead of storing and restoring its state at the time of pre-emption can be quite high. In the case of a central processor, however, the overhead is relatively small (namely storing the volatile environment of the current process), and the processor can always be regarded as pre-emptible.

Denial of condition (4) can be effected by imposing an order on resource types so that if a process has been allocated resources of type k then it may request only resources of types which follow k in the order. This ensures that the circular wait condition can never arise. The disadvantage is the constraint imposed on the natural order of resource requests, though this can be mitigated by placing commonly used resources early in the order.

An interesting example of these three ways of preventing deadlock occurred in OS/360 (Havender, 1968), and survives in modern IBM systems such as MVS. In this system, jobs are divided into 'job steps', and there is a job step initiator which is responsible for getting the resources necessary for each job step. The concurrent initiation of several job steps for different jobs is achieved by having several copies of the job step initiator. Deadlock between the copies is prevented by ensuring that each initiator always acquires resources in the order: files, memory, peripherals. Deadlock between different job steps wishing to access the same files is prevented by making the initiator acquire files for a whole job at once. It should be noted that in this case pre-emption would not be appropriate, since a job would not want its files to be tampered with by alien job steps while it was itself between job steps. Neither can any reasonable order be placed on file requests. Deadlock over peripheral allocation is prevented by forcing jobs to release resources (except files) between job steps and to re-request them for the next step if required.

(2) Deadlock detection and recovery

If the prevention policies detailed above are considered too restrictive then an alternative approach may be acceptable. This allows the possibility of deadlock, but relies on detecting it when it occurs and on being able to stage a recovery. The value of this approach depends on the frequency with which deadlock occurs and on the kind of recovery it is possible to make.

Detection algorithms work by detecting the circular wait expressed by condition (4) above. The state of the system at any time can be represented by a *state graph* in which the nodes are resources, and an arc between nodes A and B implies that there exists a process which holds resource A and is requesting resource B (see figure 8.1).

The circular wait condition is represented as a closed loop in the state graph (for example, A, B, D in figure 8.1). The detection algorithm maintains a representation of the state graph in some convenient form and inspects it at intervals for the existence of closed loops. The inspection may occur after each allocation or, since the overhead of doing this is probably too high, at fixed intervals of time.

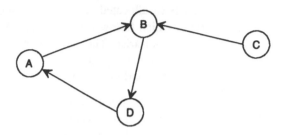

Figure 8.1 Example state graph (resources A, B and D are involved in deadlock)

Detection of deadlock is useful only if an acceptable attempt at recovery can be made. The definition of 'acceptable' can be stretched according to circumstance to include any of the following techniques, which are listed in order of increasing sophistication.

(a) Abort all deadlocked processes. This is roughly equivalent to the post office burning the occasional sack of mail whenever it gets overloaded, but is the method adopted in most general purpose systems.

(b) Restart the deadlocked processes from some intermediate checkpoint, if one exists. If naïvely applied this method may lead straight back to the original deadlock, but the nondeterminacy of the system will usually ensure that this does not happen.

(c) Successively abort deadlocked processes until deadlock no longer exists. The order in which this is done can be such as to minimise the cost of losing the investment of resources already used. This approach implies that after each abortion the detection algorithm must be reinvoked to see whether deadlock still exists.

(d) Successively pre-empt resources from deadlocked processes until deadlock no longer exists. As in (c) the order of pre-emption can be such as to minimise some cost function. Reinvocation of the detection algorithm is required after each pre-emption. A process which has a resource pre-empted from it must make a subsequent request for the resource to be reallocated to it.

It is worth remarking before we leave the subject that detection of deadlock is sometimes left to the computer operators rather than performed by the system itself. An observant operator will eventually notice that certain processes appear to be stuck, and on further investigation will realise that deadlock has occurred. The customary recovery action is to abort and restart (if possible) the deadlocked processes.

(3) Deadlock avoidance

By *deadlock avoidance* we mean the use of an algorithm which will anticipate that deadlock is likely to occur and which will therefore refuse a resource request which would otherwise have been granted. This is a notion distinct from prevention, which ensures *a priori* that deadlock cannot occur by denying one of the necessary conditions.

A tempting line of approach to devising an avoidance algorithm is as follows. Before granting a resource request, tentatively change the state graph to what it would be if the request were granted, and then apply a deadlock detection algorithm. If the detection algorithm gives the all clear then grant the request; otherwise refuse the request and restore the state graph to its original form. Unfortunately this technique will not always work since it relies on the

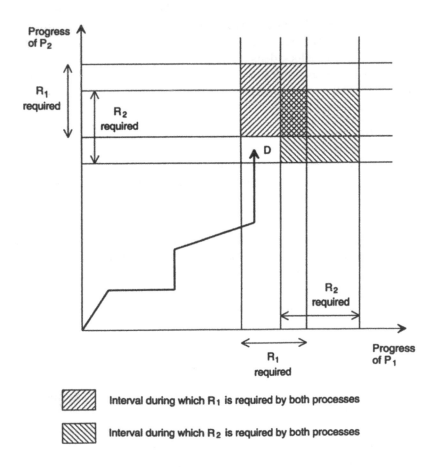

Interval during which R_1 is required by both processes

Interval during which R_2 is required by both processes

Figure 8.2 Illustration of deadlock

premise that if an allocation is going to result in deadlock then it will do so immediately. That this premise is false can be shown by study of figure 8.2 (due to Dijkstra), which illustrates a two-process, two-resource system.

The joint progress of processes P_1 and P_2 is represented by plotting a trajectory, shown in the diagram as the heavy arrowed line. The horizontal portions of the trajectory represent periods when P_1 is running, the vertical portions represent the periods when P_2 is running, and the sloping portions represent periods when both P_1 and P_2 are running simultaneously. (In a single processor configuration only horizontal and vertical portions can exist.) The trajectory is constrained from entering the shaded region on the diagram since this is an interval during which at least one of the resources R_1 and R_2 is required by both processes. The important point is that if the trajectory enters the region D then eventual deadlock is inevitable, since in that case there is no way that the trajectory can avoid meeting the shaded area (the trajectory can move only upwards and to the right, in the directions of positive progress). However, deadlock does not exist in region D itself, and so entering D would provoke no objection from any deadlock detection algorithm. Thus the use of a detection algorithm would not avoid deadlock in this case. To put it another way, a detection algorithm can see only one step ahead, whereas deadlock may be inevitable several steps ahead.

It is apparent from the above discussion that a successful avoidance algorithm must possess some prior knowledge of the possible pattern of future events so that it can spot potential deadlocks before they arise. The type of prior knowledge assumed is the feature which distinguishes one algorithm from another. We discuss next the *banker's algorithm*, which is probably the best known.

The prior knowledge demanded by the banker's algorithm is the maximum quantity of each resource which a process will require during its lifetime. We call this quantity the *claim* of a process on a resource. In batch systems this demand is quite reasonable, since job descriptions can be used to specify maximum resource requirements in advance. The algorithm allows a resource request only if

(a) the request plus the current usage is less than the claim

and

(b) after doing so there exists a sequence in which all processes can run to completion even if they all demand their full claims.

Thus before making an allocation the algorithm checks that enough resources will be left to enable such a sequence to be constructed. It has been shown (Habermann, 1969) that the work involved in making the check is proportional to the square of the number of processes in the system.

As an example of how the algorithm works, consider again figure 8.2. The claims of P_1 and P_2 are each R_1 and R_2. Before entry into region D, R_1 is allocated to P_1 and R_2 is free. Thus there are sufficient resources left to run both P_1 and P_2 to completion even if both processes demand their full claims. The appropriate sequence in this case is P_1 followed by P_2. Inside region D, R_1 is allocated to P_1 and R_2 to P_2. Thus if both processes demand their claims there is no sequence (neither P_1 before P_2 nor vice versa) in which they can run to completion. The banker's algorithm therefore refuses entry into region D by denying the request for R_2 by P_2. P_2 will be suspended, and only P_1 will be able to run. The trajectory will therefore follow a horizontal course along the lower edge of the shaded area until P_1 releases R_2. At this point the original request by P_2 for R_2 can be granted since there are now sufficient resources available to complete both processes.

It should be noted that the banker's algorithm always allows for the worst possible case (that in which all processes demand their full claims). It may therefore sometimes refuse a request because deadlock *might* ensue, whereas if the request had been granted no deadlock would in fact have occurred. For example, in figure 8.2 entry into region D is forbidden because of the possibility that P_1 might exercise its claim on R_2 and P_2 might exercise its claim on R_1. If in fact either process chooses not to exercise its claim at an awkward moment then region D would be quite safe (since the shaded areas would not occupy the positions shown), and the refusal of P_2's request for R_2 would have been unnecessarily restrictive. The tendency of the banker's algorithm towards over-cautiousness, together with the overheads of applying it, are the main drawbacks to its use.

We conclude our discussion of deadlock by considering the level in the operating system at which policies to deal with it should be implemented.

If a prevention strategy is used then all parts of the system which allocate resources operate under one or more of the constraints described earlier. The constraints can be implemented as part of the resource allocation mechanisms at the appropriate levels.

If detection is used then no alteration to the allocation mechanisms is required. The detection algorithm, which must have access to all allocation data structures, can be implemented at a high level, possibly within the scheduler itself. (The scheduler is described in later sections.)

In the case of deadlock avoidance all resource requests must be vetted by the avoidance algorithm. We shall see in the next section that all resource requests can be made via the scheduler, which thus becomes the natural place in which to implement the algorithm.

8.4 The scheduler

The term *scheduling* is generally understood to cover the questions of when to introduce new processes into the system and the order in which processes should run. As mentioned earlier these subjects are intimately related to resource allocation. In fact decisions on scheduling and decisions on resource allocation are so closely linked that it is often sensible to place responsibility for both in the hands of a single system process. We shall call this process the *scheduler*; it is also often called the *high-level scheduler* to differentiate it from the dispatcher, which is sometimes known as the *low-level scheduler*. The duties of the high-level scheduler are described below.

(1) Introduction of new processes

In a batch system, jobs awaiting execution are stored in a *job pool* which is held in secondary memory. (How they get there will be discussed in chapter 11.) The scheduler starts execution of a job by initiating an appropriate process such as compilation. The choice of which job to start next depends on the resources that each job requires (as stated in its job description) and on the current pattern of resource allocation in the system. In order to achieve high throughput the scheduler should initiate a new process as soon as resource capacity warrants it.

In a multi-access system, processes are created when users log in to the system. Each new user increases the demand on resources, and access can be refused when the number of users logged in is such as to have increased response time to the limit of acceptability.

(2) Assignment of process priorities

The order in which processes are run is determined either by the order of the processor queue or by the order in which the dispatcher selects processes from the queue. We suggested in chapter 4 that to minimise dispatching overheads the dispatcher should always pick the first eligible process in the queue; this implies that the order of the queue will be the determining factor. The scheduler is responsible for assigning priorities to processes so that when they become runnable they are linked into the appropriate place in the queue. Algorithms for determining suitable priorities will be discussed in the next section.

(3) Implementation of resource allocation policies

The policies implied here are those concerned with deadlock avoidance and with system balance; that is, with ensuring that no type of resource is either over or under-committed. Criteria for evaluating balance will be discussed in the next section.

Since the behaviour of the system is largely determined by the activities of the scheduler it is important that the scheduler should have a high priority relative to other processes. If the scheduler has top priority the dispatcher will pick it whenever it is runnable in preference to all other processes. This ensures that the system reacts quickly to changes in circumstance, particularly to changes in demand. The occasions on which the scheduler might be activated are

(1) a resource is requested

(2) a resource is released

(3) a process terminates

(4) a new job arrives in the job pool (or a new user attempts to log in)

It is instructive to note the analogy between interrupts and the scheduling events above. Both occur at unpredictable intervals, and both may cause the system to modify its behaviour. In the case of scheduling events the modifications are at a high level, affecting such global parameters as process priorities and the number of processes in the system; modifications due to interrupts are at a low level, affecting the runnability of processes and the allocation of the central processors. Interrupts may be expected to occur every few milliseconds, whereas scheduling events will probably occur only every second or so.

When the scheduler has finished its work it suspends itself by executing a *wait* operation on a semaphore; this semaphore is signalled whenever a scheduling event occurs. However, in an operating system which neither prevents nor avoids deadlock it is possible that no scheduling event does in fact occur. In this situation it is vital that the scheduler is reawakened in order to detect that deadlock prevails; this can be done by signalling the semaphore on certain clock interrupts, say every ten seconds.

The request and release of resources (the first two scheduling events above) can be implemented by providing two operating system procedures

> *request resource (resource, result)*
> *release resource (resource)*

These procedures place the necessary information about the resource concerned and the identity of the calling process in a data area accessible to the scheduler, and then signal the scheduler semaphore. The scheduler will respond according to criteria to be discussed in the next section. The second parameter of *request resource* is used to convey the result of the request, and may also give an indication of the reason for any refusal. Note that a request which is at first refused may be queued by the scheduler until the resource becomes available. In this case the request will eventually be granted and the *result* parameter of *request resource* will indicate this. The queueing operation and the associated delay are transparent to the requesting process.

A disadvantage of combining the scheduling and resource allocation functions in a single process is the overhead of process switching incurred whenever a resource is requested or released. If this overhead is thought to outweigh the gains that can be obtained from system balance and high resource utilisation, then the two functions may be separated. In this case the routines *request resource* and *release resource* perform the resource allocation functions without invoking the scheduler.

8.5 Scheduling algorithms

The general objective of a scheduling algorithm is to arrange the pattern of work performed by the computing system so as to maximise some measure of user satisfaction. This measure may differ from system to system: in a batch environment it may be total throughput or the average turnround time for a certain class of job; in a multi-access system it may be the average response time offered to users, or the response time offered to certain kinds of interaction. The scheduling algorithm used will naturally depend on the goal desired.

We start by considering algorithms which are based on the assumption that central processors are the resources of prime importance. We have already implied at the start of this chapter that in many cases this assumption is false and that other resources may also be of importance. However, by studying processor-bound systems we may gain insight into the more complex cases to be discussed later.

A general model of a processor-bound system is illustrated in figure 8.3. New processes arrive on the processor queue and are serviced by a number of processors. (We are assuming that the processors are identical.) After receiving a certain amount of service a process may be completed, in which case it

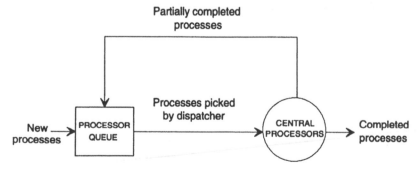

Figure 8.3 Scheduling model of a processor-bound system

leaves the system; otherwise it is returned to the queue to await further service at a later time. The model represents processes only in the runnable and running states; the omission of the blocked state of chapter 4 reflects the fact that in a processor-bound system the only significant delays which can occur are due to waiting in the processor queue. A particular scheduling algorithm is characterised by the order of processes in the queue and the conditions under which processes are fed back into it. We consider several popular algorithms next.

(1) Shortest job first

As the name implies the queue is ordered according to the running time required by each process. The algorithm is suitable only for batch systems, where an estimate of the running time can be acquired from the job description. Its aim is to minimise the turnround time of short jobs, and it is therefore best used in an environment in which short jobs form the bulk of the load. In its simplest form the algorithm allows all processes to run to completion, but a modification can be made by which a new process may pre-empt a processor if it has a running time less than that required to finish the current process. This version, known as *pre-emptive shortest job first*, is even more favourable to short jobs. Another modification, which ensures that long jobs are not delayed indefinitely, is gradually to increase the priority of a process according to the length of time that it has been in the queue.

(2) Round robin

This algorithm was developed as a means of giving rapid response to short service requests when running times are not known in advance. Each process in the system receives a fixed quantum of service before being returned to the end of the queue. The queue is therefore circular, and ordered by length of time since the last service. Processes which require lengthy service will cycle round the queue several times before being completed, while processes whose service time is less than the quantum will terminate on the first cycle. The round-robin algorithm was used in the early time-sharing system CTSS (Corbató *et al.*, 1962) and has subsequently been implemented with several variations in many other systems. Most variations have the aim of reducing the tendency of the system to collapse under heavy loading. Analysis and experience both show that if the load becomes too heavy for a given quantum size then performance is suddenly degraded. One way of overcoming this is to increase the quantum size as the number of processes rises. This increases the probability that a process will terminate within the quantum, and so reduces the overhead of process switching.

(3) Two-level queue

This is another variation of the round-robin algorithm which attempts to overcome sudden load degradation. Processes which are not completed within a fixed number of quanta are siphoned off into a 'background' queue which is serviced only if there are no other processes in the system. The background queue may itself be treated on a round-robin basis with a larger quantum, or it may be simply first come, first served. The two-level system is often used in mixed batch and multi-access environments, where the longer batch processes tend to sink into the background and are serviced only when no terminal initiated processes are present. The algorithm can of course be generalised to a *multi-level system* if this is considered appropriate.

A more complex version of this algorithm may be found in EMAS (Rees, 1981) where process scheduling was based on four different priorities. High priority queues were serviced more frequently than low priority queues, in ratios such as (16:10:5:1). Processes changed priority according to their current position within a *category table*, movement within which was based on previous process resource usage, including consumption of memory as well as of CPU time. Highly interactive processes tended to stay in a high priority category, whereas those which exhibited characteristics more appropriate to a background or batch process quickly migrated to a low priority category. The values in the category table were easily changed.

The optimal values of the parameters of the round-robin algorithm and its descendants, such as quantum size and when to move processes to a background queue, are difficult to determine analytically (but see Coffman and Denning, 1973, and Sauer and Chandy, 1981, for some attempts). Approximations may be found by simulation, and adjusted after experience of real life running conditions.

These algorithms form the basis of most popular scheduling policies. Other algorithms and variations can be found in the excellent survey by Coffman and Kleinrock (1968). One particular variation of note is to allow the inclusion of externally specified priorities. The effect is that processes with high external priority receive a better service than would be the case with the pure form of the algorithm. This enables users with tight deadlines or VIP status to obtain better response from the system, though they may be charged more for the privilege.

Systems in which central processors are not the sole resources of importance can be described by the model shown in figure 8.4. This model differs from that of figure 8.3 by the inclusion of the blocked state, in which processes wait for resource requests or I/O transfers. The addition of this state greatly increases the complexity of the model. Firstly, the state is characterised not by

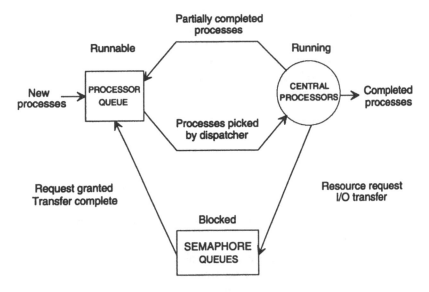

Figure 8.4 General scheduling model

a single queue but by a multiplicity of queues associated with the various semaphores which cause blocking to occur. Secondly, processes move from the blocked to the runnable state after events such as the signalling of a semaphore which occur at unpredictable intervals. The movement of processes between queues can be studied for different scheduling strategies either by formal analysis or by simulation (Svobodova, 1976), though the complexity of the model makes both techniques difficult to apply.

The reader will see from figure 8.4 that one of the aims of a scheduling algorithm could be to minimise the number of transitions from the running state to the blocked state. Since the transitions due to I/O transfers are outside its control it follows that the algorithm should minimise the number of resource requests which are refused. This implies that processes should be introduced into the system only if their likely resource demands can be satisfied by the resources currently available. This policy is more easily implemented in batch systems, where maximum resource demands can be specified in advance, than in multi-access systems, where demands are virtually unpredictable. An example of batch implementation was the Atlas operating system, in which jobs were divided into three classes: short jobs, requiring little processor time and no esoteric peripherals; magnetic tape jobs, whose name is self-explanatory; and long jobs, comprising the rest. The scheduler attempted to maintain at least one job of each class in the system at any given time.

It is worth noting that policies such as this will not necessarily result in high resource utilisation. The reason is that a process is unlikely to use, throughout its life, all the resources of which it has given notice. The resources claimed, and allowed for by the scheduler, may therefore lie idle for considerable periods. If higher utilisation is required the scheduler must make policy decisions on resource allocation not only when introducing a new process but also when each resource request or release occurs. The criteria for making such decisions and for assigning process priorities are generally empirical; we discuss a few of them next.

(1) Processes which possess a large number of resources may be given high priority in an attempt to speed their completion and regain the resources for redeployment elsewhere. The danger of pursuing this strategy is that large jobs might monopolise the machine or that users may generate dummy resource requests in order to gain favourable treatment. This latter danger can be avoided in a batch system by ensuring that jobs with small resource requirements are selected for running in preference to others.

(2) Processes which possess a large number of resources could have further requests granted whenever possible. The justification is similar to that above, and again there is a danger that large jobs might monopolise the system.

(3) Memory allocation in paged machines can be performed according to the working set principle described in chapter 5.

(4) Operating system processes should have priorities which reflect the urgency of the functions they perform. The scale will range from the scheduler itself at the top to such processes as the incremental file dumper at the bottom. Most system processes will have higher priorities than user processes.

(5) As a special case of (4), peripheral device handlers should have high priority. In general the faster the device the higher should be the priority of the associated handler. This ensures that peripherals are kept busy as much as possible, thereby reducing the potential of I/O bottlenecks. If spooling is used then the spoolers should also have high priority.

(6) Unless deadlock prevention measures are in force all resource requests should be subjected to a deadlock avoidance algorithm.

(7) The overhead in making scheduling decisions should not be out of proportion to the ensuing gains.

The considerations above may be used to modify one of the processor scheduling algorithms described earlier. The result will be an algorithm in which process priorities are continually being updated according to the pattern of resource demand and the state of the system. The performance of such an algorithm is difficult to gauge except by observation; it can often be substantially improved by quite minor alterations to its parameters. An interesting example of such an improvement arose in the DECSystem-10. In an early version of the scheduling algorithm processes which re-entered the runnable state after being blocked while awaiting terminal I/O were placed on the end of the first-level processor queue. This procedure was subsequently changed so as to place these processes on the front of the first-level queue. The improvement in response to multi-access users was dramatic.

We may summarise this section by saying that the number of possible scheduling algorithms is very large, but that at present we have no means of selecting an optimal algorithm for a specific case other then by experiment. Analysis and simulation can be of some help, but their value is restricted by the complexity of most systems.

8.6 Process hierarchies

We saw in section 8.4 that the scheduler is responsible for initiating new processes. Thus in a sense the scheduler is the parent of all processes introduced into the system. Moreover, it is responsible for the welfare of its offspring in that it governs policies of resource allocation and influences the order in which processes are selected by the dispatcher. This parental role need not be restricted to the scheduler; it can be extended to other processes by allowing them the capability to

(1) create subprocesses

(2) allocate to their subprocesses a subset of their own resources (the resources being returned when the subprocess terminates)

(3) determine the relative priority of their subprocesses

The effect is to enable the creation of a hierarchy of processes with the scheduler at the head. Thus the natural form of the process structure is no longer the simple list of chapter 4, but a tree as shown in figure 8.5. The tree is partially threaded by the process queue, which links all the nodes (processes) which are currently runnable.

The advantages of a hierarchical organisation are twofold. First, it allows a process which performs several independent tasks to create a subsidiary process for each task so that the tasks may be executed in parallel. Of course nothing is gained on a machine with a single central processor since only apparent concurrency can be achieved, but when several processors are available real gains may result.

Second, it allows several versions of the operating system, each oriented towards a different application, to run independently and in parallel. The different versions, or subsystems, will each be based on the facilities provided by the system nucleus (see chapter 4), but may use different algorithms for the implementation of the higher system functions which appear in the outer

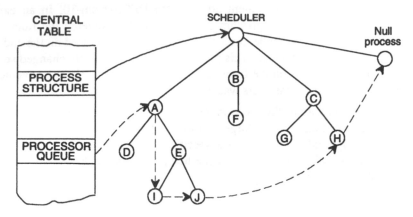

Figure 8.5 A process hierarchy

layers. Thus each subsystem is a particular version of our 'onion', though all subsystems have the same core. The various subsystems each implement a virtual machine which is suitable for a particular class of user, and all the virtual machines coexist in the same physical configuration.

As an example consider figure 8.6, which illustrates a situation in which two different subsystems are responsible for batch and on-line work respectively. The performance of the two subsystems is governed by the resources and relative priorities allocated by the scheduler; within these constraints each subsystem can control its subordinate processes according to any appropriate algorithms. Within the batch subsystem, for example, all I/O may be spooled and user processes ordered on a shortest first principle; within the on-line subsystem I/O may be unspooled and processes ordered in a round robin. One can imagine an extension of the hierarchy in which, for instance, the batch subsystem is divided into further subsystems which handle different classes of job.

One advantage of the subsystem arrangement is the coexistence of different virtual machines. Another is the ability to develop new versions of an operating system while the old version runs in parallel. Against this must be set the loss of global control over resource allocation which results from the way in which resources are passed up and down the process structure. Resources which have been allocated to a subsystem or to an inferior process, and which are not being used, cannot be transferred elsewhere in the system unless they are first returned to a common ancestor. Since processes are free to allocate subsets of their resources as they wish there is no guarantee that the overall pattern of resource utilisation will in any way be optimal.

The assignment of priorities by a process to its offspring can also create problems. Unless some restrictions are imposed it is possible for a process to

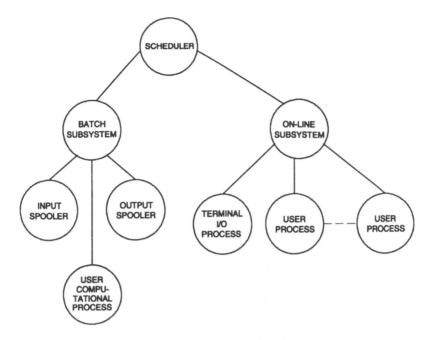

Figure 8.6 Example of multiple subsystems

gain an unfair scheduling advantage by delegating its task to a subprocess to which it assigns a very high priority. One form of restriction which will overcome this problem is to insist that all priorities are assigned relative to that of the parent process, and that the range over which relative priorities may vary successively decreases at each level down the hierarchy. For example, suppose that in figure 8.5 the range of relative priorities at the top level is 0-99, and at the second level is 0-9, and so on. Then if the priority of process B is 20, no subprocess of B may have a priority outside the range 20 ± 9. This implies that if the priority of process A is greater than 29 then B cannot gain any advantage over A by splitting itself up into subprocesses. If the priority of A is greater than 39 then all subprocesses of A will be guaranteed priority over subprocesses of B.

In the situation shown in figure 8.6 the relative priorities assigned by the scheduler to the batch and on-line systems effectively determine the response of the system to the two classes of job. A large difference in priority between the subsystems will ensure that one class of user always gains preference over the other; a small difference will result in competition for the central processor(s) on more equal terms. The relative priority of processes within each subsystem is, as mentioned earlier, a matter for the subsystem concerned.

One of the earliest operating systems displaying a hierarchical process structure was that on the RC-4000 computer (Hansen, 1970). The nucleus of this system was referred to as the Monitor, and the head of the hierarchy, which corresponded to our scheduler, was called the Basic Operating System. Up to 23 processes (the restriction was for reasons of space) could exist in the structure, and resources were passed from parents to offspring as described above. One difference between the RC-4000 system and the one we have outlined is that parents could not assign priorities to their children; all processes had equal priority except in so far as they were selected by the dispatcher on a round-robin basis.

A limited hierarchy is also provided by the IBM VM (Virtual Machine) operating systems (Seawright *et al.*, 1979). The structure is normally limited to three levels: at the root is the VM operating system itself, at the next level may occur any of a number of other operating systems (acting as subsystems), and at the lowest level are the user tasks. The operating systems which run at the second level provide various virtual machines on the same configuration. The dispatcher works according to a two-level round-robin discipline which can be modified by assigning relative priorities to each subsystem.

The implementation of a hierarchical process structure requires the provision of the system procedures

> *create process* (*name, relative priority*)
> *delete process* (*name*)
> *start process* (*name*)
> *stop process* (*name*)

The function of *create process* is to set up a process descriptor for the new process and link it into the process structure. *start process* adds the process descriptor to the processor queue; that is, it marks the process as eligible to run. *stop process* and *delete process* perform the inverse functions, and allow a parent to control its children. Children may of course terminate of their own accord, in which case the use of *stop process* is unnecessary. All four procedures manipulate process descriptors or the processor queue, and should therefore be implemented within the system nucleus. The procedures *request resource* and *release resource* described in section 8.4 are amended so as to invoke the parent process rather than the scheduler. The parent process is thus made responsible for allocation to its offspring.

8.7 Control and accounting

The previous sections have been concerned with the allocation of resources on a time scale which is comparable with job running times. We now turn our attention to longer term aspects of resource allocation, that is to such questions as charging for resource usage, estimating and influencing the pattern of demand, and ensuring that all users receive an appropriate proportion of the computing facilities available. These matters are usually described by the term *resource control*. Strictly speaking, resource control is the concern of the computer manager rather than the operating system designer, but unless the designer provides the appropriate tools the manager is impotent. In particular the designer must provide tools for measurement, since without measurement no control is possible.

The aims of resource control depend on the installation concerned. Broadly speaking installations are of two types: *service* and *in-house*. The purpose of a service installation, such as exists in a bureau, is to provide computing facilities for a number of paying users. No restrictions, other than the ability to pay, are placed upon users; indeed it is in the interests of management to sell as many facilities to as many users as possible. Resource control is thus reduced to *accounting*, that is, to recording the amount of each chargeable resource used and billing each user accordingly.

An in-house installation on the other hand is owned by a single company, university, or other institution, and provides facilities only to members of that institution. Because of budgetary constraints the manager has the problem of dealing with a demand for service which nearly always exceeds the installation's capacity. Unlike a bureau no profit is gained from providing service, and so the option of increasing capacity to meet demand is not usually open. Thus the manager must ration the resources available according to the relative needs or importance of the various users. Resource control in this case provides a tool for discrimination between users. It must fulfil the dual function of accounting for resources and ensuring that no users exceed their ration.

It should be clear that the control mechanisms required for service installations are a subset of those required for in-house installations. We shall therefore concentrate on the latter.

(1) Restriction of access

Access to facilities which entail heavy resource usage can be denied to certain classes of user such as junior programmers or students. Again, users working in multi-access mode might be restricted to editing and small scale testing, while batch users are allowed free range of all facilities.

(2) Rationing

A rationing policy may be either long or short term, or a combination of both. Short-term rationing applies a limit to the amount of resource, such as processor time or memory space, which can be used by a single job. In long-term rationing a budget is given to each user indicating the amount of resources which can be used in a given period, for example, a week or a month. Attempts by a user to exceed the ration result in job abortion or refusal of access to the system.

Both methods of control can be implemented by maintaining an accounting file which contains the following information for each accredited user of the system.

(1) The user identification. This is an 'account number' quoted by the user when logging in or at the head of a job description. It serves to identify the user to the system.

(2) A password known only to the user and to the system. This is presented by the user as proof of identity. (Passwords are not normally required in batch systems, since their secrecy is difficult to maintain.)

(3) A 'permission vector' in which each bit represents the permission to use a certain facility. Permission is granted only if the appropriate bit is set.

(4) The resource limits for a single job.

(5) The budget for the current accounting period.

(6) The resources still outstanding in the budget for the current period.

The details of how control is applied vary from system to system. In batch-oriented systems the outstanding resource balance is debited at the end of each job, and jobs are accepted by the scheduler only if the balance is positive. An alternative is to accept a job only if its stated resource requirements are less than the current balance; this prevents a user exceeding the ration by running a large job when the balance is almost zero. In a multi-access system the balance may be debited at regular intervals during a terminal session and the user forcibly logged off (after an appropriate warning) if the balance reaches zero.

Rationing may be applied to each resource separately or, more commonly, the usage of each resource may be compounded through some specified charging formula into some kind of global resource consumption units. In this case the relative weights given to each resource in the charging formula are chosen so as to reflect the resource's importance or scarcity value. An example of such a charging formula is

number of units used $= (K_1 \times P) + (K_2 \times C) + (K_3 \times M) + (K_4 \times W)$

where

$P =$ central processor time in seconds

$C =$ terminal connect time in seconds

$M =$ memory occupancy, that is the integral over processor time of the number of page frames used

W = number of disk transfers

$K_1 ... K_4$ = multipliers chosen by management

It is worth noting that the parameters K_i in the charging formula can be altered in order to influence the way in which users work. For example, a dramatic increase in the charge for terminal connect time would encourage users to make greater use of batch facilities, while an increase in the memory occupancy charge might be an incentive to writing small jobs.

Another important feature of a rationing policy is that the total allocated amount of each resource should be related to the amount of the resource which the system can supply in the given time period. The amount allocated and the amount in supply need not be equal, since there is a good chance that most users will not consume their entire allocation; the degree of safe over-allocation can be gauged by experience. In the case of global charging formulae the allocation and supply are more difficult to match, for if all users decided to use their allocation in the form of the same resource then the system could not cope. In practice the existence of a large user population makes this eventuality unlikely.

More sophisticated rationing policies (for example, Hartley, 1970, McKell *et al.*, 1979) may employ different charging rates at different times of the day. This encourages use of the machine at unpopular times and gives a more even distribution of the work load. Similarly, charges may vary according to the external priority that a user has requested for his or her work.

The system designer's responsibility is to provide the tools for implementing policies such as those just described. These tools include

(1) routines for administering the accounting file

(2) mechanisms for measuring resource usage

(3) mechanisms for refusing facilities to users who have overdrawn their budgets

The measurement of resource usage is a function which is distributed throughout the system at the points where resources are allocated. It can be greatly facilitated by the provision of suitable hardware, such as a counter in the disk controller to record the number of transfers. A real time clock is of course essential to accurate measurement. Measurements on an individual process can be stored as part of the process descriptor, and statistics on total system usage can be gathered in a central file. The latter figures can be regarded as an indicator of system performance and used as a basis of comparison and enhancement.

Consideration should perhaps also be given to the question of whether operating system overheads should be charged to the user. On the one hand it can be argued that the operating system is acting on behalf of the user, and that the user should therefore be charged. This would have the beneficial side-effect of encouraging users to write programs in such a way as to minimise system overhead, by avoiding redundant file accesses for example. On the other hand the overheads will vary according to the current load, and it might be considered unfair to charge a user more simply because the machine is busy or because his job interacts unfavourably with some other job which happens to be present at the same time. It could also be argued that the ordinary user should not be expected to acquire the detailed knowledge of the operating system that would be needed for him to modify his work to reduce overheads. A possible compromise is to charge the user for all system activities, such as I/O handling, performed specifically on his behalf, but not to charge for activities such as process switching which are outside his control. However, even this leaves some areas subject to dispute; paging traffic for example is dependent both on the user, who can increase the locality of his memory references, and on the current pressure of demand for memory. Ultimately, decisions in this field are necessarily arbitrary, and must be left to the individual designer.

8.8 Summary

In this chapter we have seen how policies for resource allocation and scheduling can be implemented in a single process which we called the scheduler. We have described how the functions of the scheduler can be extended to other processes, thus establishing a hierarchical process structure. The nucleus of our paper operating system has been enlarged by the inclusion of procedures for creating and deleting processes. The mechanisms for allocating resources and for measuring resource usage are distributed throughout the system at the

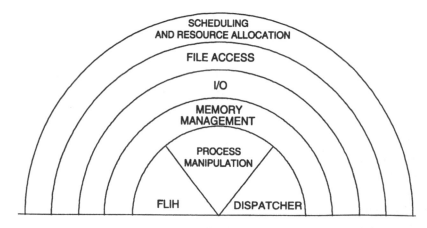

Figure 8.7 Current state of the paper operating system

levels appropriate to the resources concerned. The current state of our system is as shown in figure 8.7.

The additional data structures are

(1) a record of available resources

(2) for each process a list of resources allocated to it, pointed to from the process descriptor

(3) if deadlock detection is employed then a representation of the state graph

(4) if deadlock avoidance is employed then a record of resource claims and allocations

(5) a possible elaboration of the processor queue to include several levels

(6) a possible modification of the process structure which turns it into a tree

(7) an accounting file.

9 Protection

We have already alluded several times to the fact that processes within a computing system must be protected from each other's activities. We have introduced mechanisms at various points in our paper operating system which ensure that the memory, files, and resources belonging to a process cannot be accessed by another process except in a controlled manner. The mechanisms have been distributed throughout the system in such places as the memory addressing hardware, file directories, and resource allocation procedures, and have functioned more or less independently of each other. In this chapter we take a closer look at the subject of protection as a whole and indicate how it is possible to implement protection mechanisms on a unified system-wide basis.

9.1 Motivation

The motivation for protection mechanisms in a multi-user computing system may be summarised as follows.

(1) Protection from faults

When several processes, possibly working for different users, are executing on the same machine it is clearly desirable that faults in any one of them should not be allowed to affect the running of the others. Few users would tolerate a system in which every process had to be guaranteed fault-free before they could be confident that their own work would be run without interference. Mechanisms must therefore be devised to erect 'fire walls' between the different processes in the system. Protection from faults applies not only to user processes but also to the operating system itself. If the operating system can be corrupted by faults in a user process then it is unlikely to perform well (or at all) for very long.

Protection is desirable even in the case of a single user with a private machine. In this situation protection can be an aid to debugging by limiting the propagation of errors and localising the original source. Even when programs are fully debugged protection can minimise the damage caused by hardware malfunction or operator error. These considerations apply even more forcefully in multi-user systems.

(2) Protection from malice

At a time when computers are increasingly being used for storing and processing databases, many of which contain confidential information, it is essential that the security of data can be guaranteed. The guarantee may be required for commercial reasons, as in the case of an installation which provides a service to users with divergent interests, or it may be required for reasons of privacy and even legality. For example, employees of government agencies such as the tax office or social security must be prevented from accessing confidential personal records without authorisation. The safeguards required for data apply equally to programs. For example, a company which has invested a great deal of money in developing a program which it intends to sell or hire will not be happy if its customers or competitors are able to copy the program and install it elsewhere. Similarly, the tax office would be dismayed to find that one of its employees had modified a program so that he had paid no tax for the past five years.

An operating system itself is a collection of programs and data which must be protected from malice. It is not difficult to imagine a user modifying an unprotected system so that his or her jobs are always scheduled first, or to avoid being charged for the resources used.

If protection were simply a matter of isolating all processes from each other then adequate mechanisms could readily be devised. Unfortunately, processes may well have legitimate grounds for wishing to share resources, access common data, or execute the same programs. A worthwhile protection system must therefore allow legitimate sharing while preventing unauthorised interference. It is the coexistence in a computing system of elements of both co-operation and competition which makes protection a problem.

9.2 Development of protection mechanisms

Protection in the elementary sense of totally excluding unauthorised users from the system can be achieved by requiring that a user present some proof of identity when logging in or submitting a job. The user generally does this by quoting an account number, which is used in charging for the resources used, and a password known only to the user and to the operating system. The account number and the password are checked against the system accounting file, as described in section 8.7. This technique can be made more secure by encrypting the user's password when first assigned, via a one-way encryption algorithm, and storing the encrypted version in the accounting file. When the password is subsequently presented to the system it is encrypted using the same algorithm, and compared with the copy in the accounting file. This makes security of the accounting file much less of a problem; although the password could be determined by exhaustive search, choice of an encryption algorithm which takes a significant time to run can make this an impracticable way of breaking security.

Provided that the password is made inaccessible to users in some way, and provided that each user keeps his or her own password secret, then entry to the system can be made by authorised users only. Unfortunately, this latter proviso is difficult to enforce in practice since users have a habit of disclosing their passwords, either inadvertently or through a misplaced sense of generosity. In batch systems in particular it is difficult to keep passwords secret since they may have to be stored in files as part of some job description. Consequently many batch systems do not demand passwords at all; any security is implemented by restricting access to the input device. Even in multi-access systems where the users observe strict secrecy it has been proved that a determined intruder, through a process of inspired trial and error, can eventually discover a valid password and penetrate the system. (If the system insists on passwords of a reasonable length, and allows any character to be part of a password rather than just letters and digits, this possibility can be minimised.) We shall not discuss this topic any further here, but shall concentrate for the rest of this chapter on the protection measures that can be applied once users have gained some form of access (legitimate or otherwise) to the system.

A rudimentary form of protection can be achieved by including in the hardware of the host machine a *mode switch* and a pair of *base and limit registers*. The mode switch governs the ability to execute privileged instructions as described in section 4.1, and the base and limit registers demarcate the area of memory accessible to a process when in user mode (see section 5.3). Information which is resident in main memory is protected by the base and limit registers, whose values can be altered only when the processor is in supervisor mode; information on backing store is protected by virtue of the fact that I/O instructions are privileged and thus all data transfers can occur only via the operating system. Validation of the transfers can be achieved by using information held in the file directories when the files are opened and closed, as described in chapter 7.

This form of protection was found in most computers of the mid 1960s (for example the ICL 1900 series). It is unsatisfactory in that it is an 'all or nothing' solution to the protection problem: a process either has no privileges (executing in user mode) or all privileges (executing in supervisor mode). Thus, for example, processes executing any system procedures have the same absolute privileges, irrespective of whether they need them. Furthermore, sharing of data or programs among processes is possible only by making their memory spaces overlap, in which case the processes are completely unprotected from each other.

A more flexible protection scheme can be implemented if the host machine is equipped with segmentation hardware (see section 5.3). In this case the address space of each process is divided into logical segments, and each segment can be given a particular degree of protection (such as execute only or read only) by incorporating a protection indicator into its descriptor. The situation is illustrated in figure 5.5. The memory addressing hardware checks all accesses to the segment to ensure that the protection specified in the descriptor is not violated.

Since each process references its segments through its own set of segment descriptors (held in its segment table) it is possible for two processes to reference the same physical segment through descriptors which have different protection indicators. This allows segments to be shared among processes with different access rights. Figure 9.1 shows an example in which a process *A* reads information which is deposited in a buffer by process *B*. The buffer appears as a segment in the address spaces of both *A* and *B*; its descriptor in process *A* specifies read only access while its descriptor in process *B* allows write access. Both descriptors point to the same location in memory.

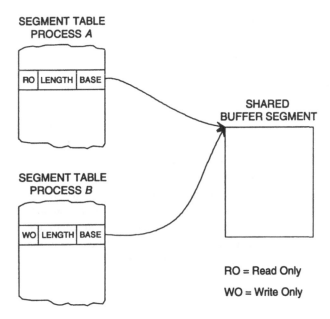

Figure 9.1 Segment sharing with different access privileges

Although this scheme is an improvement on the previous one it still does not provide us with adequate protection. The reason is that the access rights which a process has for a segment remain unchanged throughout the process's lifetime. This means that whatever program or procedure the process is executing it maintains constant privileges over all its segments. (An exception to this is when the process enters supervisor mode, when it assumes absolute privileges over all segments.) A preferable arrangement, not provided for by the scheme above, is that a process should at all times possess only those privileges which it needs for the activity in which it is currently engaged. This philosophy of 'minimum necessary privilege' is essential to the aim of limiting the effects of erroneous or malicious processes.

As an example consider again processes A and B of figure 9.1. If use of the buffer is extended to include two-way communication between the processes then both A and B require write access to it. This means that each process has the ability to write to the buffer even at those times when it is supposed to be reading, and thus the information in the buffer cannot be guaranteed against malfunction in either process. What is required is that the access privileges of A and B for the buffer should be dependent on whether they are currently engaged in sending or receiving information. Thus when either process is executing a procedure for sending information it should have write access to the buffer, but when it is executing a procedure for receiving information the access should be read only.

As a result of this discussion we introduce the idea of a *domain* of protection (other terms are *sphere*, *context* and *regime*) in which a process executes. Each domain defines a set of privileges or *capabilities* which can be exercised by a process executing in it. A change of capabilities can be achieved only by a transition from one domain to another; we naturally insist that such transitions are strictly controlled.

Primitive examples of domains are the supervisor and user modes of execution mentioned earlier. When a process executes in supervisor mode its capabilities include the right to execute privileged instructions and to reference the whole memory; when it is in user mode its capabilities are restricted to the use of non-privileged instructions and to accessing only its own memory space. For reasons discussed earlier this two-domain system is inadequate for our purposes: what we have in mind is a more complex arrangement in which a number of domains define a large variety of capabilities and in which a process runs in the domain which contains just those capabilities which allow it to transact its legitimate business. We shall examine in the following sections how such an arrangement can be implemented.

It is worth noting at this point that capabilities for all objects which require protection can be expressed in terms of capabilities for memory segments. Access to a system data structure can, for example, be expressed in terms of access to the segment containing it while permission to operate a peripheral device depends on access to the segment containing the device descriptor. (Some computers, such as the VAX and many microprocessors, incorporate device addresses within the overall address space; in these computers access to devices can be controlled in exactly the same way as access to memory.) This observation leads to a significant simplification of protection schemes since it allows all protection to be performed by means of segment capabilities, which in turn can be implemented as part of the memory addressing mechanisms. This approach is followed in the schemes described below.

9.3 A hierarchical protection system

In this section we describe the protection scheme implemented in MULTICS (Graham, 1968; Schroeder and Saltzer, 1972; Saltzer, 1974). MULTICS was one of the earliest systems to treat protection in a generalised way and has inspired several similar systems such as VME on the ICL 2900. Our description is somewhat simplified, but will serve to illustrate the ideas behind a hierarchically organised protection scheme.

Domains in MULTICS are called *rings*, and are ordered so that each ring contains a subset of the capabilities of the one inside it. Conceptually the arrangement can be viewed as shown in figure 9.2, where the progression from the outermost (high numbered) rings to the innermost (low numbered) rings bestows successively greater privileges. The reader will see that this is a refinement of the supervisor/user mode system of protection, which can in fact be considered as a two-ring system.

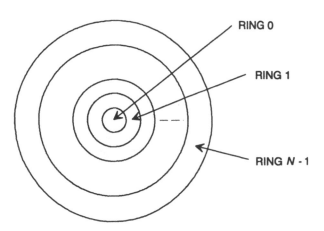

RING 0

RING 1

RING *N* - 1

Figure 9.2 Rings of protection

A ring in MULTICS is a collection of segments, and for the moment we shall consider that each segment is assigned to one and only one ring. Procedures which require a large number of privileges reside in segments in inner rings, while procedures needing fewer privileges, or which cannot be trusted to be error-free, are contained in segments in outer rings.

In order to identify the ring to which a segment belongs, its segment descriptor is extended to include a field holding the ring number. The program counter is similarly extended to identify the ring in which the current process is executing (that is, the ring number of the segment from which it is executing instructions). The protection indicator in the segment descriptor includes flags which denote whether the segment can be written, read, or executed (see figure 9.3). A process executing in ring i has no access whatever to segments in ring j, where $j < i$; its access to segments in ring k, where $k \geq i$, is governed by the access indicators of the segments concerned. In other words access to inner rings is prohibited, while access to outer rings is subject to the access indicators. An attempt by a process to cross a ring boundary by calling a procedure in a different ring results in the generation of an error trap. The trap causes entry to a special trap handler which performs certain checks on the transfer of control. These checks will be described in a moment.

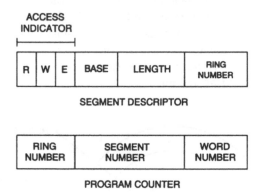

Figure 9.3 MULTICS segment descriptor and program counter

The mechanism described above is adequate for the provision of hierarchical protection. However, the fact that a segment is assigned to only one ring leads to inefficiencies arising from the large number of procedure calls across ring boundaries. A more flexible arrangement, adopted in MULTICS, is to allocate each segment to a set of consecutive rings known as its *access bracket*. The ring field of the segment descriptor then contains two integers $n1$ and $n2$ which specify the lowest and highest rings of the access bracket. A call by a process executing in ring i to a procedure in a segment with access bracket $(n1, n2)$ does not now cause a trap so long as $n1 \leq i \leq n2$, and in this case control remains in ring i.

If $i > n2$ or $i < n1$ a trap is generated, and the corresponding trap handler must decide whether the call is to be allowed. (The trap handler may be a procedure in ring 0 or, as in MULTICS, it may be largely integrated into the memory addressing hardware.) The case $i < n1$ represents an *outward call*, that is, a transfer of control to a ring with lesser privileges, and can therefore always be allowed. However, the parameters of the call may refer to segments which are inaccessible to the called procedure because of its inferior status. In this case the parameters must be copied into a data area accessible to the called procedure.

A call in the reverse direction ($i > n2$) is more difficult to handle. Since the call represents a transfer of control to a ring with higher privileges care must be taken that the caller cannot in any way cause the called procedure to malfunction. A first step in this direction is to allow calls only from rings which are not too far distant from the access bracket of the called procedure. An integer $n3$ ($n3 > n2$) held in each segment descriptor is used to define the limit of the segment's call bracket; a call from ring i, where $i > n3$, is not permitted. Further, each segment possesses a list (which may be empty) of the entry points, or *gates*, at which it may be called. The trap handler checks that all inward procedure calls are directed to one of these gates, and generates an error if this is not the case. The trap handler also records on a stack the return point and ring number corresponding to the call. Returns across rings are validated against the top of the stack to ensure that a procedure cannot be tricked into returning to a ring lower than that prevailing before the call. The parameters of an inward call also require validation in case they refer to segments which should be protected against the caller.

The disadvantage of hierarchical protection systems such as the one outlined above is that if an object must be accessible in domain A which is not accessible in domain B then A must be higher up the hierarchy than B. This implies that everything accessible in B must necessarily be accessible in A. This can be regarded as falling a long way short of the goal of giving a process the minimum necessary privileges at all times. However, the various layers of protection do to some extent mirror the layers of construction of an operating system, and therefore form a naturally attractive way of reinforcing operating system structure. The designers of the MULTICS system claimed that the hierarchical structure does not in practice impose embarrassing constraints, and that satisfactory protection can be provided. In the next section we shall examine an alternative which does not depend on a hierarchical organisation.

9.4 General systems

In the hierarchical protection scheme described above the capabilities which can be exercised by a process are implicit in the number of the ring in which it is executing. Furthermore, transfers of control from one ring to another imply either an extension or a reduction of the capabilities currently available. In a non-hierarchical system, on the other hand, transfers in control between domains are accompanied by quite arbitrary changes in a process's capabilities. The set of capabilities belonging to a process in a particular domain is known as its *capability list*: a change of domain implies a change of capability list. In a hierarchical system the new capability list is always either an extension or subset of the old, while in a non-hierarchical system there is no obvious relationship.

An abstract model for a general protection system (Graham and Denning, 1972; Saltzer and Schroeder, 1975) is an *access matrix* (figure 9.4) which denotes the capabilities of various *subjects* for all system objects which need protection. A subject is a pair (*process, domain*), so each row in the matrix represents the capability list of a particular process executing in a particular domain. When a process changes domain it becomes a different subject and its capability list is represented by a different row of the access matrix. In general subjects require protection from each other, and so subjects are also regarded as objects.

OBJECTS

	Subjects			Files		Devices	
	S1	S2	S3	F1	F2	D1	D2
S1		stop delete		read write	.		seek
S2			stop		update	write	
S3				delete	execute		

Figure 9.4 Part of an access control matrix

Associated with each object is a *controller* which is entered whenever the object is accessed. Depending on the type of object concerned the controller could be implemented in hardware or software: typical examples might be those shown in the table.

Type of object	Controller
File	Filing system
Segment	Memory addressing hardware
Peripheral	Device handler

The controller is responsible for ensuring that a subject possesses the appropriate capability for the type of access requested. A particular protection scheme is characterised by the choice of subjects and objects, by the capabilities denoted by the elements of the access matrix, and by the way in which capabilities can be modified or transferred.

The model includes all the elements of a general protection system, but an efficient implementation for a wide range of object types is difficult to envisage. However, if as suggested in section 9.2, the range of objects is restricted to memory segments and if a process may change domain only when entering a new segment then implementation can be achieved in terms of the memory addressing hardware. Two approaches to such implementation are described below.

The first approach (Evans and Leclerc, 1967) is to regard a capability, which takes the form (*access indicator, segment base, segment length*), as equivalent to a segment descriptor, and to identify the capability list of a process with its segment table. A change of domain by a process implies a change of segment table. A consequence of this approach is the destruction of the notion of a process-wide address space, since a process will change address space according to the domain in which it is executing. Some difficulties are also encountered in parameter passing: for example, a recursive procedure requires a separate segment table for each level of call, the successive tables giving access to the parameters appropriate to each level.

An alternative approach is that adopted in the Plessey 250 computer (Williams, 1972; England, 1974). We shall describe this implementation in some detail since it illustrates the way in which memory addressing schemes based on capabilities can be expected to some extent to replace the more traditional schemes discussed in chapter 5. (See Fabry, 1974, for strong advocacy of such a development.)

A capability in the Plessey 250 consists of the access indicator, base address and limit address of a particular segment. The capabilities of the current process are held in a set of program accessible processor registers known as *capability registers*, and program addresses are specified by giving the number of a capability register and an offset. The desired memory location is obtained by adding the offset to the base address held in the capability register. The limit address and access indicator are used to check memory and access violations.

The reader might wonder at this point whether the set of capability registers is not conceptually the same thing, apart from differences of speed, as the traditional segment table. The distinction is that the allocation of capability registers is under local program control and the programmer, or compiler, is free to reallocate the registers as they see fit. By contrast, segment table entries

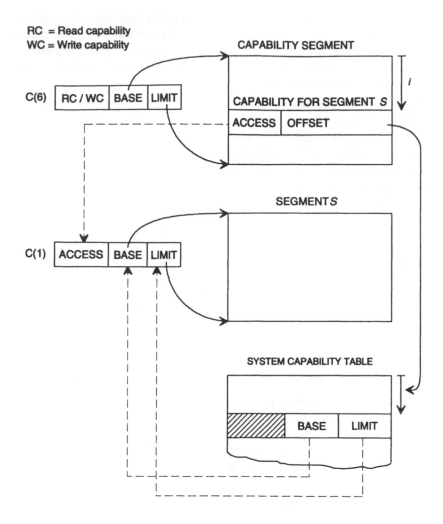

RC = Read capability
WC = Write capability

Figure 9.5 'Load capability' operation (C(1) := C(6) + i)

are allocated by an operating system on a global basis, and once allocated they remain fixed.

Since it is economically feasible to provide only a small number of registers, the capabilities of a process are also stored in a capability segment in memory and loaded into the capability registers as required. Thus the capability segment currently accessible to a process represents its capability list and defines its domain of execution. Access privileges 'read capability' and 'write capability', which are distinct from the normal 'read' and 'write' and which apply only to the capability segment, are used to prevent ordinary data items being treated as capabilities. This prevents capabilities being manufactured in data segments and loaded into capability registers. By convention, capability register C(6) is used to address the capability segment of the current process, and register C(7) is used to address the segment containing the code being executed.

A further refinement is necessary in order to facilitate the sharing of segments among processes. In the scheme as described the relocation in memory of a shared segment would involve a change to the corresponding capabilities in the capability segments of all the processes concerned. To avoid this the base and limit addresses of all segments in memory are contained in a *system capability table*, and all stored capabilities refer to segments individually through this table. Relocation of a segment thus involves an alteration only to the system capability table and not to the entries in the individual capability segments. Figure 9.5 illustrates the process of loading capability register C(1) with a capability for segment S which is contained in the ith entry of the capability segment.

It should be noted that the system capability table is itself a segment, addressed by a special capability register, and is accessible only to certain parts of the operating system which are concerned with memory management. It is invisible to all other processes, which can regard the capabilities in the capability segments as pointing directly to the segments concerned.

A process may change domain (that is, change its capability segment) only if it possesses a special 'enter' capability for the capability segment of the new domain. Figure 9.6 illustrates the way in which a process executing a program MAIN calls a procedure SUB in a different domain. Initially C(6) addresses the capability segment for MAIN and C(7) holds an 'execute' capability for the segment containing the program code of MAIN. The process possesses in C(0) an 'enter' capability for the capability segment of SUB, which in turn contains in its ith location an 'execute' capability E for the code segment of SUB. A procedure call specifying C(0) and offset i results in C(6) being replaced by the 'enter' capability in C(0), and C(7) by the 'execute' capability E. Thus C(6) and C(7) now point to the appropriate capability and code segments in the new domain. A 'read capability' privilege is added to C(6) to enable the called procedure to read its own capabilities, and the previous values of C(6) and C(7) are placed on a stack for retrieval on the subsequent return. Neither the caller nor the called procedure has access to the other's capabilities, except for those capabilities which may be passed as parameters in registers C(1) to C(5). The scheme therefore affords complete protection between mutually suspicious procedures.

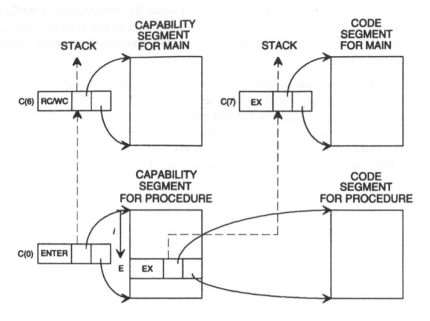

Figure 9.6 Changing the domain of execution
(CALL C(0) + i)

9.5 Conclusion

We have seen in this chapter that the need for protection is a natural consequence of a multi-user environment. With the advent of large-scale databases
and a growing concern over privacy, security and reliability, this need is likely
to become more pressing. Although protection has traditionally been provided,
to a greater or lesser extent, by a variety of mechanisms at various points in the
system it is now becoming possible to take an integrated approach. Given
suitable hardware we would wish to include in our paper operating system a
protection scheme similar to one of those described above.

10 Reliability

In section 2.3 we stated that one of the desirable features of an operating system is reliability; indeed an unreliable system is of very little use. In this chapter we examine more closely what is meant by reliability, and discuss ways in which the reliability of an operating system can be increased. We shall see that reliability is not an 'add-on' extra, but a requirement which must be considered from the earliest stages of system design.

10.1 Objectives and terminology

It will be apparent from the preceding chapters that an operating system is a complex piece of software which is expected to perform a variety of functions for a diverse set of users. It is important to the users that these functions are performed correctly, and one of the principal objectives of the system designer is to ensure that this is the ease. The task of the designer is made more difficult in that the finished product will not be operating in a perfect world: it is likely to be subjected to a large variety of circumstances which could adversely affect its functioning. Such circumstances include malfunction of the hardware of the host computer, errors in procedure by the computer operators, and illegal or meaningless requests supplied by the user. An operating system should continue providing service, possibly of a degraded nature, even in the face of such adverse circumstances.

These remarks lead us to define the *reliability* of an operating system as the degree to which it meets its specifications in respect of service to its users, even when subjected to unexpected and hostile conditions. This definition emphasises that reliability is a relative rather than an absolute concept: no system can be totally reliable since, to take an extreme example, it would be impossible to provide service in the face of simultaneous failure of all hardware components of the computer. A highly reliable operating system will continue to meet its specification even under great pressure from hardware malfunction or user error; a less reliable system may depart from the specification when subjected only to a single meaningless request.

The level of reliability which should be achieved by an operating system depends, of course, on the reliance its users place on it. Heavy reliance, as in a system which controls a space capsule or monitors the condition of hospital patients, demands high reliability; lesser reliance, as in a system for document preparation and retrieval, requires less reliability. Since (as we shall see later) high reliability often incurs high costs, the system designer should aim at a level of reliability which is commensurate with the reliance of its users. (It is interesting to note, however, that the reliance of users may be influenced by the reliability of the system.)

The concept of reliability should not be confused with that of *correctness*: the notions are related but distinct. An operating system is *correct* if when running in a specified environment it exhibits a specified (desired) behaviour. Correctness is certainly a desirable attribute of an operating system, but it is an insufficient condition for reliability. This is because demonstrations of correctness, whether by testing or by formal proof, rely on assumptions about the environment which are generally invalid. Such assumptions typically concern the nature of inputs and the correct functioning of hardware, and may be quite unjustified in practice. Putting it another way, the environment in which a system operates rarely matches that which is assumed in the demonstration of correctness.

Correctness is not only an insufficient condition for reliability, but, perhaps more surprisingly, it is also an unnecessary one. Parts of an operating system may be incorrect in that the algorithms governing particular processes may not produce the required effect, but the system can still operate reliably. As an example, consider a filing system in which the *close* routine in some circumstances omits to record the length of a file in the corresponding directory entry. Provided that the file terminates with a recognisable 'end of file' mark, the I/O routines can still read the file successfully, and the system will perform reliably even in the face of the incorrect operation of one of its components. This example illustrates the use of redundant, or superfluous, information to conceal and recover from errors, a technique to which we shall return later.

The reader should not assume from this that correctness is unimportant. It may be neither a necessary nor a sufficient cause for reliability, but it certainly helps. An operating system which is correct is likely to be more reliable than one which is not. It would be bad practice indeed for a designer to depend on reliability mechanisms to conceal the effects of known deficiencies, or even to justify lack of effort towards correctness. The proper course is to attempt to produce a system which is correct with respect to specified assumptions, and at the same time to design reliability mechanisms to cater for those occasions on which the assumptions are invalid. We shall examine these complementary approaches in later sections.

At this point we introduce three more items of terminology. We define an *error* to be a deviation of the system from its specified behaviour. Thus an error is an event; examples are the allocation of unshareable resources to two processes, or the deletion of the directory entry for a file which is still being used. An error may be caused by a hardware malfunction, by the unanticipated action of a user or operator, or by a deficiency ('bug') in one of the programs within the system. In all cases we use the term *fault* to mean the cause of an error. When an error occurs it is probable that some items of information within the system are corrupted. We refer to such corruption as the *damage* caused by the error; damage can of course result in faults which lead to further errors. We shall see that one of the means of achieving high reliability is to limit the damage that can be caused by an error, and hence limit the propagation of errors throughout the system.

From the foregoing discussion we can see that efforts towards producing a highly reliable operating system should be concentrated on the following areas

(a) *fault avoidance*: elimination of faults in the design and implementation stages; that is, production of a correct system

(b) *error detection*: detection of errors as soon as possible in order to reduce the damage caused

(c) *fault treatment*: identification and elimination of any fault which produces an error

(d) *error recovery*: assessment and repair of damage resulting from an error

In the following sections we shall deal with each of these in turn.

10.2 Fault avoidance

As we have seen, faults in a computer system may stem from the hardware, from operator or user incompetence and ignorance, or from 'bugs' in the software. Ways of avoiding each of these types of fault are discussed next.

(1) Operator and user faults

We shall say little about operator and user generated faults other than that they can never be eliminated; all that can be hoped for is a reduction in their number by means of appropriate training and user education programmes, and by the design and development of improved user interfaces (see chapter 11).

(2) Hardware faults

The most obvious way of reducing the incidence of hardware faults is to use the most reliable components which can be obtained within the overall cost constraints. Hardware designers use several methods of enhancing reliability, ranging from the obvious – using individually reliable components – to more complex techniques which incorporate some form of error detection and recovery within each subsystem. Error detection is usually based on the recording or transmission of redundant information, such as parity bits and checksums;

recovery is often attempted by repeating the operation which gave rise to the error. Examples of this technique are magnetic tape and disk drives which are designed to repeat operations a limited number of times if either parity or checksum problems occur. Retrying operations is of course useful only for transient faults (that is, faults which are due to temporary conditions such as interference or dust particles); permanent faults will still result in errors.

Another technique which is often used in data transmission is the use of error detecting and correcting codes, in which redundant information transmitted with the data provides a means of recovery from certain transmission errors. Yet another technique is that of *majority polling*, in which several (usually three) identical components are supplied with the same inputs and their outputs are compared. If the outputs differ the majority verdict is taken to be correct, and the component producing the minority verdict is noted as being suspect. A component which is repeatedly in the minority is assumed to be faulty and can be replaced. Majority polling is an expensive reliability technique since it relies on replication of components and it is normally used only when really high reliability is essential.

The aim of all the techniques discussed is to *mask* the hardware faults from the software which runs on it. That is, faults may be present in the hardware but their effects are concealed from the software, so that as far as the software is concerned the hardware appears fault free. We shall see in section 10.6 that the notion of masking can be extended into the operating system itself, so that errors which occur in one level of the system are hidden from the levels outside it.

(3) Software faults

There are several complementary approaches to reducing the incidence of software faults. We discuss three of the principal ones next.

The first approach is to adopt management practices, programming methodologies and software tools which are a positive aid towards producing a fault free product. In the mid 1960s it was believed in some quarters that the larger the piece of software to be produced the more programmers should be assigned to it. IBM's experience with huge armies of programmers on OS/360 exploded this myth, and it is now realised that indiscriminate application of manpower is likely to create more problems than it solves. The grouping of programmers into small teams, popularly known as 'chief programmer teams', is now considered a better way of organising software production. Each team is responsible for a module of software which has precisely defined external specifications and interfaces, and within the team each member has a well-defined function, such as coding, documentation, or liaison with other teams. Detailed consideration of such organisational practices is beyond our present scope: a revealing and entertaining account of various pitfalls is given by Brooks (1975).

The way in which programmers actually go about writing programs can have considerable influence on the quality of the finished product, in terms of coherence, comprehensibility and freedom from faults. Several programming methodologies have been advocated, the most widely known being *structured programming* (Dahl *et al.*, 1972; Wirth, 1971) and its various derivatives (for example Jackson, 1975; Yourdon *et al.*, 1979; Yourdon, 1989). Structured programming has been sufficiently publicised elsewhere for us not to go into detail here: the reader who wishes to know more is referred to the accounts above, or to Alagic and Arbib (1978). A more recent development is object-oriented programming, about which there is much literature (for example Wiener and Pinson, 1988). See also Fagan (1976) for further attempts to improve reliability.

The software tools which are of most help in creating a fault-free product are probably an editor, a macro-assembler, and a compiler for a suitable high-level language. We have already remarked in section 4.2 that the only parts of an operating system which need to be written in assembly language are those which are intimately bound up with the host hardware, namely parts of the nucleus and the I/O device handlers. The use of a high-level language for the rest of the system speeds up the production of useful code and facilitates the elimination of faults. It is sometimes said that high-level languages are unsuitable for writing operating systems since the object code produced is less efficient in execution than the corresponding handwritten code. There are at least three counters to this view: first, that a good optimising compiler can often produce better code than a good assembly language programmer; second, that areas of residual efficiency can if necessary be optimised by hand; and third, that reliability is at least as important a goal as efficiency.

The second general approach to reducing the incidence of software faults is to attempt to prove, by more or less formal means, that all programs in the operating system, and all their interactions, are correct. This is a formidable task, which for large systems is beyond the current state of the art. However, pioneering work by Floyd (1967), Hoare (1972) and Dijkstra (1976) has opened up the possibility of such proofs being possible in the not-too-distant future. Even now, a great deal of confidence in the correctness of a system can be inspired by proofs of correctness for some of its component programs.

The most popular approach to proving program correctness (Alagic and Arbib, 1978; Hantler and King, 1976; Hayes, 1987) is to formulate assertions (usually expressed in predicate calculus) which are to be true at various stages of program execution. The proof then proceeds inductively from the assumption of the initial assertion to verification that execution of the program statements does indeed make the subsequent assertions true. The chief difficulties encountered are the formulation of appropriate assertions, and the rather laborious step-by-step proof of their truth.

The third approach to eliminating software faults is by means of systematic testing. Testing has always been a prime method of detecting faults, but there is surprisingly little agreement on an appropriate methodology. Ideally, one would like to test a program on all possible inputs, but this is clearly impractical; all one can hope for is that the test data chosen will reveal all remaining faults. There is no general way of selecting test data to do this, though several pragmatic guidelines have been proposed. One such guideline is to select test data which will exercise all possible paths through the program. Another is to select data which lie at the extremes of the allowable ranges: for example, zero is an obvious choice in any situation where the inputs can range over the positive integers.

The difficulty of testing is compounded when a large number of programs are to be executed by several interacting processes, as is the case in an operating system. Not only must each program be tested, but so must the interfaces between different programs and processes. The only hope of doing this at all successfully is to keep the interfaces as simple as possible.

We can summarise this discussion by saying that none of the approaches outlined above – programming methodology, formal correctness proofs, and testing – can be relied on to yield a fault-free product. The techniques are still evolving, but it is fair to say that a combination of these three approaches can even now substantially raise one's confidence in the correctness of the software produced.

10.3 Error detection

The key to error detection is *redundancy* – that is, the provision of 'superfluous' information which can be used to check the validity of the 'main' information contained within the system. The term 'redundancy' reflects the fact that the information used for checking is redundant so far as the main algorithms of the system are concerned. We have already seen in the last section how redundant information such as parity bits and checksums can be used for error detection in the hardware sphere. Coding is also a useful means of error detection, and in some cases can be used for recovery as well. As mentioned before, errors detected by the hardware may be masked by the hardware itself, or they may be reported to the operating system by means of traps into the first-level interrupt handler (section 4.4). Examples of the latter type of error are arithmetic overflow, memory violation, and protection violation. The actions which can be taken by the operating system will be described later in this chapter.

Error detection may also be undertaken by the operating system itself. A common form of checking is for processes to check the consistency of the data structures they use. An example of this might be for the processor queue to be held as a doubly linked list and for the scheduler to trace the links both forwards and backwards whenever it accesses the queue. The redundant information provided in this case is the set of backward links: only the forward ones are required for the main scheduling and dispatching algorithms. Another example is the checking of table modifications by maintaining in the table a checksum of all its entries. When an entry is modified the effect on the checksum can be predicted by calculation. If the checksum after modification does not correspond to that predicted then an error has occurred during modification.

A generalisation of this form of checking (Randell, 1975) is to associate with each major action of a process an *acceptance test* which can be used as a criterion of whether the action has been properly performed. The acceptance test is a Boolean expression which is evaluated (as part of the process execution) after the action is completed. If the result is 'true' the action is considered to have been performed correctly; if it is 'false' an error has occurred. The acceptance test can be as stringent as is deemed necessary; it will be formulated to check for those errors which the designer feels are most probable. As an example consider the action of the scheduler in periodically modifying process priorities and re-ordering the processor queue. The acceptance test for this operation may be simply that the process descriptors in the re-ordered queue are indeed in priority order. A more stringent acceptance test contains the additional constraint that the number of descriptors in the queue is the same as before, thus guarding against the inadvertent detachment or duplication of a descriptor. There is of course usually a trade-off between the stringency of an acceptance test and the overhead of performing it, a trade-off which applies to all error-detection mechanisms. The designer must weigh the costs, in capital equipment or performance degradation, against the benefits accruing. Unfortunately, it is often the case that neither costs nor benefits can be accurately measured.

So far we have dealt only with errors which occur within a single hardware or software component. Errors which occur at the boundary between components are more difficult to detect, but some advantage can be gained from checking the credibility of any information passed across a boundary. For example, some procedure parameters can be checked to see that they fall within an appropriate range, and it may be possible to check that messages passed between processes conform to some established protocol.

We conclude this section by noting that early detection of an error is the best way of limiting the damage which may be caused, and of limiting the wasted processing which may result. The capability of an operating system to react to errors soon after they occur can be greatly enhanced by the provision of suitable hardware protection mechanisms. Thus the protection mechanisms discussed in chapter 9 can make an important contribution not only to the security of an operating system but also to its reliability. (See Denning, 1976, for greater elaboration of this point.)

10.4 Fault treatment

Treatment of a fault first involves locating it, and then repairing it. As any systems programmer will testify, detection of an error and location of the corresponding fault are not at all the same thing. An error may have several possible causes, located in either the hardware or the software, and none of them may be apparent. One of the main aids to fault identification is the detection of errors before their cause is obscured by consequent damage and further errors. Thus the early detection of errors, as indicated at the end of section 10.3, is of prime importance.

In some cases it may be possible to take the easy option of ignoring the fault altogether, but this involves assumptions about the frequency of the errors it can cause and the extent of their damage. For example, it may not be considered worthwhile to attempt to locate a transient hardware fault until the frequency of errors that it causes crosses some threshold of unacceptability (Avizienis, 1977; Nelson, 1990). Usually, however, it is important that a fault be located and dealt with. The search for a fault will generally be directed by the investigator's understanding of the system structure. If this is incomplete, or if the fault has affected the structure, then the investigator's task is difficult indeed.

One way of helping the investigator is for the system to produce a trace, or log, of its recent activity. Events recorded in the log might be process activations, procedure entries, I/O transfers, and so on. Unfortunately the amount and detail of information recorded must be very large if the log is to be of practical value, and the overhead of recording it can be very high. Some advantage can perhaps be gained from making the trace optional, so that it need be switched on only when there is reason to believe that the system is malfunctioning. It is also worth while making the trace selective, so that only those parts of the system which are suspect need log their activities. This of course requires a subjective judgement (itself prone to error), of which are the suspect parts.

Once a fault has been located its treatment involves some sort of repair. In the case of hardware faults repair usually comprises the replacement of a faulty component. This may be done manually or automatically, depending on the ability of the hardware to locate its own faults and 'switch out' a faulty component. Manual replacement may involve taking the entire system out of service for a time, or, preferably, it may proceed in parallel with continued service, possibly at a degraded level. Repair of a disk drive, for example, should not interrupt normal service if other drives are available, but replacement of a printed circuit board in the central processor of a single CPU system will probably require a complete shutdown and restart.

Faults in software components arise from deficiencies in design and implementation, or from corruption caused by previous errors. (Unlike hardware, software does not usually suffer from faults due to ageing.) Removal of a design or implementation fault usually involves the replacement of a (hopefully small) number of lines of program, while a corrupted program can be replaced by a backup copy held elsewhere. The repair of corrupted data is a topic we shall leave to the next section, which deals with error recovery generally. As with hardware, one would hope that software components can be replaced without the need to close down the entire system, and the system should be designed with this in mind.

10.5 Error recovery

Recovery from an error involves assessment of the damage which has been caused, followed by an attempt to repair it. Damage assessment may be based entirely on *a priori* reasoning by the investigator, or it may involve the system itself in performing a number of checks to determine what damage has occurred. In either case, assessment (like fault identification) will be guided by assumed causal relationships defined by the system structure. An error in updating a file directory can, for example, be expected to damage the filing system but not the process structure or the device descriptors. There is of course a danger that the system structure, and hence any assumed relationship, will itself be damaged, but the probability of this happening is greatly reduced if appropriate hardware protection mechanisms are employed (as suggested in section 10.3).

The usual approach to repairing damage is to reverse, or *roll back*, the affected processes to a state which existed before the error occurred. This approach relies on the provision of *recovery points* (or *checkpoints*) at which sufficient information is recorded about the state of the process to allow it to be reinstated later if necessary. The information required is at least the volatile environment and a copy of the process descriptor; it may also include a copy of the content of the memory space used by the process. The interval between recovery points determines the amount of processing which is likely to be lost when an error occurs. The loss of information after an error can be reduced by *audit-trail* techniques, in which all modifications to the process state are logged as they occur. Error recovery then consists of rolling back to the last recovery point and then making the state changes indicated by the audit log. Audit-trail techniques are analogous to the incremental dump of a file system, described in section 7.5; in fact the incremental dump can be viewed as a particular audit-trail mechanism.

Recovery points and audit-trails imply the recording of all state information and all modifications to it. An interesting alternative (Randell, 1975) is the *recovery block* scheme, in which the only state information recorded is that which is actually modified. Since the scheme also includes elements of error detection and treatment we feel it is worthy of brief description.

A recovery block is a section of program with the following structure

> **ensure**   *acceptance test* **by**
>   *primary alternate*
> **elseby**
>   *secondary alternate*
> **elseby**
>   *other alternate*
> **elseby**
>   .   .
>   .   .
>   .   .

The primary alternate is the program fragment which is normally executed; the other alternates are used only if the primary alternate fails. Success or failure of an alternate is determined by the execution of the acceptance test (see section 10.3) associated with the block. Thus execution of the recovery block first involves execution of the primary alternate, followed by execution of the acceptance test. If the test passes, which is the normal case, the entire block is deemed to have been executed successfully. If the test fails, the process state is restored to that which existed before the primary alternate was executed, and the secondary alternate is then executed. The acceptance test is again used to determine success or failure, and further alternates are invoked as necessary. If all alternates fail then the block as a whole is said to fail, and recovery has to be made by invoking an alternate block if there is one (recovery blocks may be nested to any depth), or by restarting the process if not.

The alternates within a recovery block can be viewed as software spares which are automatically utilised whenever the primary alternate fails. Unlike hardware spares the alternates are not of identical design, and usually employ different algorithms. The primary alternate employs the most efficient or otherwise desirable algorithm for fulfilling the function of the block; the other alternates employ less efficient algorithms, or algorithms which fulfil the desired function in only a partial, but still tolerable, fashion. Failure of an alternate is regarded as an exceptional occurrence (akin to an error due to a transient hardware fault), and the alternate is replaced only for the current execution of the block. It is wise, however, to log all failures, so that residual design and programming faults can be recognised and eliminated.

The recovery block scheme relies for its operation on the ability to restore a process state whenever an acceptance test fails. The ease of doing this depends on whether the process concerned has interacted with other processes during execution of the block. If it has not, restoration of its state reduces to restoring the prior values of all program variables and registers which have been changed. This can be effected by means of a 'recovery cache' (Horning *et al.*, 1974), a portion of memory in which values are stored before being modified. Only those values which are modified need be stored in the cache, and values which are modified several times need be stored only once. Failure of an alternate causes the restoration of values from the cache before the next alternate is tried; success of an alternate leads to the deletion of values from the cache, since the modifications can now be regarded as valid. The nesting of recovery blocks is catered for by organising the cache in a manner similar to a stack.

The case of process interaction within a recovery block is more difficult to handle. A possible approach (Randell, 1975) is to regard any interaction between two processes as a 'conversation' between them. If one of the processes has to be rolled back during a conversation then so must the other, since the information transmitted in the conversation may have been erroneous. Thus neither process may proceed beyond the end of a conversation until both have passed acceptance tests at its conclusion, and failure or either acceptance test results in the rollback of both processes to the start of the conversation. The idea can be extended to simultaneous conversations between several processes.

This description of the recovery block scheme has been necessarily brief, but the reader will recognise that it combines several aspects of fault tolerance discussed earlier. Error detection is achieved by means of acceptance tests; fault treatment is effected by the provision of alternates; and recovery is based on the cache mechanism. A more detailed description of the scheme is given in the quoted references.

10.6 Multilevel error handling

In the previous few sections we have described various error handling techniques. In this section we suggest how these techniques can be incorporated into the layered structure of our paper operating system.

The principal aim is to mask from each level of the operating system the errors which occur at levels below it. Thus each level of the system is to be as far as possible responsible for its own error recovery, so that to levels above it appears fault free. The idea is an extension into the operating system of the hardware error masking discussed in section 10.2. In cases where masking is impossible, errors in a lower level which occur while performing some function for a higher level should be reported to the higher level in an orderly fashion (for example, by a specific error return). The higher level may itself then be able to perform some kind of recovery, thus masking the error from higher levels still. Those errors which cannot be masked at any level must, of course, eventually be reported to either the user or the operator. At the lowest level of the system, errors which are detected by the CPU hardware, but cannot be masked, are reported to the nucleus by means of error traps into the first-level interrupt handler (section 4.4).

As an example of what we mean, consider a user process which wishes to open a file. The process invokes the filing system by calling the *open* routine (section 7.6), which in turn invokes the I/O system by calling the DOIO procedure (section 6.2) to read the user directory from disk. The required I/O transfer is eventually initiated by the disk device handler. In the event of a parity error a first level of masking may be provided by the hardware of the disk controller itself, which is probably designed to detect such an error and re-read the corresponding block. If a few retries fail to correct the situation the error will be reported to the device handler by means of the device status register, which is set by the controller at the end of the transfer. The device handler may attempt to mask the error by re-initiating the entire operation, but if this is unsuccessful the error must be reported back to the open routine in the filing system (by means of an error return from DOIO). Within the filing system recovery is possible if another copy of the directory exists elsewhere: the I/O system can be requested to read the backup copy. If for some reason this also fails, or if the filing system is not sufficiently well designed to maintain backup directories, then the error can be masked no longer and must be reported to the user.

Another error which could appear during the file opening operation is the corruption of a queue pointer in the disk device request queue. This may be due to hardware malfunction or to a programming fault. If, as suggested in section 10.3, the queue is organised as a doubly linked list and the queue manipulation routines trace both forward and backward links, then loss of the IORB for the directory transfer can be avoided. Damage to the pointer is repaired by the queue manipulation routines themselves, thus masking the error from the device handler and hence from the filing system and the user process.

By contrast it is interesting to note what will probably happen if the request queue is only singly linked, so that the queue manipulation routines cannot detect the error, let alone mask it. In this case the IORB will become detached from the queue, and the value of the semaphore request pending (section 6.2) will be inconsistent with the number of requests in the queue. One of two things will happen next. The first possibility is that the device handler will assume that a successful wait operation on *request pending* implies the existence of an IORB in the queue. It will then remove a non-existent IORB from the queue, interpret the resulting garbage as a valid I/O request, and provoke untold further errors. The other possibility is that the device handler will check that the request queue does indeed contain at least one valid IORB and, finding that it does not, will report this back to the DOIO procedure. In this case the error will have been successfully masked from the user, since the IORB can be regenerated. The lesson, however, is to include as much error detection and recovery capability as possible at each level, thus avoiding the potential of serious damage. Further examples of multilevel error handling along these lines are given in a description of the reliability of the HYDRA system (Wulf, 1975).

Some errors, of course, should not be masked, since they are indicative of a gross fault in the user program. These errors are not system errors, but user errors: the operating system's responsibility is to do nothing more than report them to the user. An example is arithmetic overflow, which is detected by the processor and reported to the system nucleus by the first-level interrupt handler. The interrupt routine in the nucleus can readily identify the culprit as the current process for the processor concerned, and the process can be aborted with an appropriate error message. (It can be argued that masking of an arithmetic overflow is possible, for example, by setting the affected location to the largest number that can be represented. However, we consider such action to be undesirable, since it is likely to lead to further errors which will obscure the original fault.) Other errors which should not be masked are memory and protection violations resulting from execution of user programs. The latter could, however, be logged, since they may be indicative of deliberate attempts to break down system security.

10.7 Conclusion

In this chapter we have described techniques for enhancing the reliability of an operating system. As computers intrude into many more areas of human activity, and as reliance on them increases, reliability will be of paramount importance. The techniques we have described, although still subject to considerable refinement, form a basis for achieving the reliability required. So far as our paper operating system is concerned, we note that its layered structure is well suited to the multilevel error handling suggested in section 10.6, and that we therefore expect, by using the techniques described, to achieve high reliability.

Finally we refer the reader who wishes to make a more detailed study of reliability to the excellent surveys by Denning (1976), Randell *et al.* (1978); see also Shooman (1984).

11 The User Interface

In the preceding chapters, we have described how a general purpose operating system can be constructed. At present our operating system exists somewhat in a vacuum, since we have not yet specified how we can inform it about the jobs that we want it to do. The next step is to manufacture an interface between the user and the operating system so that the user can tell the system what is required of it. The interface can also be used to present information, such as resource requirements, about each job so that the system can optimise performance in the ways described earlier. Of course, communication between user and system is not all in one direction; we must also construct a complementary interface through which the system can tell the user what it has been doing.

11.1 Some general remarks

The interface between user and system implies the provision of a language, however primitive, in which communication can take place. The nature of the language is heavily dependent on the type of operating system concerned; languages for interactive use often differ widely from those used in batch systems. The reason for this is that the nature of interactive working allows a user the opportunity to direct the course of the work in person, and to respond to system actions as they happen. In a batch system, on the other hand, the user has no further control over the job after submitting it; hence explicit instructions must be given in advance as to what course of action is to be followed, possibly specifying alternatives in cases where it is not possible to foresee precisely what eventualities may occur.

A consequence of the two styles of working is that languages used for batch operation have tended to be more complex and powerful than those used in multi-access. Indeed in the latter case the language may be no more than a set of commands which can be used as directives to the operating system. Such a language is often termed a *command language*, as opposed to the more general *job control language* used in a batch environment. Many operating systems attempt to provide both batch and multi-access control in a single language (such as IBM's CMS (REXX), DEC's VMS (DCL), and the various flavours of the UNIX shell program). In these cases multi-access users can find themselves employing only a subset of the complete job control language although, with the increasing use of predefined files of commands to perform common tasks, the distinction between batch and multi-access work is becoming less clearly defined (such command files falling between the two extremes).

A common desirable feature of both command and job control languages is that they should be easy to use. We shall say more about this later.

11.2 Command languages

The example below, loosely based on DCL in VMS, illustrates several points which should be borne in mind when designing a command language. The example is the record of a short terminal session; responses typed by the system are shown underlined in order to distinguish them from commands typed by the user. The figures in parentheses refer to the notes following.

```
                                                         Notes

Username: EAGER                                           (1)
Password:                                                 (2)

   Last interactive login on Sunday,  3-JAN-1993 09:45
   Last non-interactive login on Friday,  1-JAN-1993 00:41

$ edit prog.for                                          (3)
   .
   .
   .
*EXIT
USER2:[EAGER]PROG.FOR;1 4 lines

$ fortran prog                                           (4)
Undefined statement label
   [ 100] in module PROG$MAIN at line 1
USER2:[EAGER]PROG.FOR;1 completed with 1 diagnostic
   .
   .
   .
$ edit prog.for                                          (5)
   .
   .
   .
*EX
USER2:[EAGER]PROG.FOR;2 4 lines

$ fort prog                                              (6)

$ link prog                                              (7)

$ run prog                                               (8)
Hello world
FORTRAN STOP                                             (9)

$ lo
```

EAGER   logged out at 3-JAN-1993 11:52:05

(1) Request to log on, quoting account EAGER.

(2) Echoing of password is suppressed.

(3) Create short FORTRAN program in file PROG.FOR; details of editing omitted, editing commands terminated with EXIT.

(4) Attempt to compile program. Note that file type FOR is omitted, since system supplies it as a default.

(5) After failed compilation, edit program to make correction.

(6) Compile program successfully.

(7) Link program with run-time library.

(8) Run program; output directed to the terminal.

(9) Log out of system.

Points arising from the example are as follows.

(a) To avoid unnecessary typing, sensible and unambiguous abbreviations should be allowed wherever possible (for example, FORT and LO are abbreviations of FORTRAN and LOGOUT respectively). The full command can be typed whenever the user is unsure of a particular abbreviation.

(b) Commands should preferably be mnemonic, so that they are easy to remember and easy to guess at if forgotten (for example LOGOUT, RUN and EDIT).

(c) In commands which take parameters defaults should be supplied whenever possible (for example in the FORTRAN command the default second component of the file name is FOR; the default I/O device when the program is run is the terminal). The judicious choice of defaults can save a lot of tedious typing.

(d) It should be possible to perform commonplace activities with very little effort. For example, the FORTRAN command in this example could usefully be extended to link and run the program automatically, given a successful compilation.

(e) The format of commands should be as relaxed as possible (for example the number of spaces between command elements is arbitrary).

(f) It should always be obvious whether or not the system is ready to receive another command (this is signified by the dollar sign at the beginning of each line).

(g) The system should give sufficient information to users to indicate what is happening, but not so much that they are drowned in verbiage. Some systems (such as VMS) allow users to tailor messages to match their level of expertise.

It has to be said that not many systems provide even the small amount of help suggested above; for example, UNIX (for historical reasons) concentrates on very terse commands with a minimum of feedback from the system. The UNIX equivalent of the above would be something like the following; it is actually remarkably verbose by UNIX standards!

```
                                                          Notes
login: rde
Password:
Last login: Sun Jan 03 11:11:57
% vi prog.f                                                (1)
    .
    .
    .
:wq
"prog.f" 5 lines, 71 characters
% f77 prog.f                                               (2)
prog.f:
MAIN:
"prog.f", line 1: Error: missing statement number 100
Compilation failed
% vi prog.f
    .
    .
    .
:wq
"prog.f" 5 lines, 71 characters
% f77 prog.f
prog.f:
MAIN:
% a.out                                                    (3)
Hello world
% logout
```

(1) Create short FORTRAN program in file **prog.f**; details of editing omitted, editing commands terminated with **:wq**. Note that the editor is invoked with a short (two character) name; this is not an abbreviation. The command to exit is (incidentally) also rather opaque.

(2) Attempt to compile program. Note that the compiler is invoked with another terse command.

(3) By default, the compiled program is left in a file called **a.out**; the user types the name of this file to run the program.

11.3 Job control languages

In early batch operating systems, such as the IBSYS system for the IBM 7090 series, job control was achieved by the insertion of *control cards* at various points in the program and data. The control cards had some particular identifying feature (in IBSYS a '$' in column 1) and were interpreted by the operating system as instructions as to what to do with the cards which followed. The disadvantages of this arrangement are threefold.

(1) The sequence of operations to be performed cannot be altered in the light of the success or failure of previous steps.

(2) Control information is scattered throughout the input, which is logically unappealing and renders it prone to error.

(3) The control cards need some special combination of characters to identify them; this combination must therefore never occur in programs or data. (One way round this problem is to provide a special control statement which alters the identifying feature for all subsequent control cards to some other combination of characters. This option is available in IBM JCL.)

In some systems (for example VMS) this type of job control still exists; of course, most modern systems no longer use decks of punched cards, but files containing sequences of system commands. Even then, it is likely that some simple test and branching facilities will be provided in order to overcome disadvantage (1) (in VMS there are IF and GOTO commands). However, many systems require that all job control information should be located in a *job description* at the start of a job. The job description is effectively a program written in a job control language which controls the passage of the job through the computing system.

The control information to be specified in a job description can be classified as follows.

(1) Accounting information

This usually consists of the job name and the user identity. The latter can be checked against the list of bona fide users in the accounting file, and any chargeable resources used by the job can be debited against the corresponding account.

(2) Scheduling information

This generally consists of a specification of the maximum amounts of various resources which the job will use. Systems such as IBM's MVS, where jobs are broken up into separate job steps, may require resource specification for each step. The information required is that which can be used by the high-level scheduler for

(a) deciding which job to start next

(b) allocating priorities

(c) avoiding deadlock

(d) terminating jobs which exceed their resource limits

Typical resource specifications will include memory occupancy, processor time, and output limits.

Other scheduling information that might be included is

(a) a request that a job have a certain priority;

(b) a requirement that a job be run after some other job – sequencing specifications like this are useful in cases where a job is dependent on a file left by some other job;

(c) an indication of special peripheral requirements (for example, three magnetic tape drives).

(3) I/O information

This is the information used in stream-based systems to associate streams with physical I/O devices and/or files (readers who wish to remind themselves about streams should refer to section 6.1). In non-stream systems, this section of the job description is used to request the assignment of I/O devices and/or files for the job. Specifications of character codes and block sizes may also be included under this heading.

(4) Procedural information

This part of the job description actually tells the operating system what the user requires it to do. Some job control languages may allow nothing more than a simple sequence of directives; others may provide more powerful facilities as discussed next.

As an example, there follows a simplified job in IBM JCL.

```
//RDE1    JOB EAGER,'TEST',TIME=(10,30),REGION=1024K    (1)
//*
//COB        EXEC   PGM=IKFCBL00                         (2)
//SYSIN      DD     DSN=EAGER.SOURCE.COBOL(PROG1)        (3)
//SYSPRINT  DD     SYSOUT=*
//SYSLIN     DD     DSN=EAGER.TEMP.OBJECT(PROG1)
//
```

The four kinds of information are present, although slightly mixed and in a different order:

    (1) Job statement; contains accounting information (account name EAGER) and scheduling information (time limit and memory required).

    (2) Procedural information; this statement invokes the COBOL compiler program.

    (3) I/O information; these statements specify the location of the source file, the compiler listing file, and the compiled object file.

The power of a job control language is largely determined by its facilities for expressing procedural information. Some of these facilities are discussed below.

    (1) *Macros.* A macro facility allows users to specify complex actions by single commands. Any sequence of job control statements may be defined as a named *macro* (or *catalogued procedure*), and invoked simply by quoting the macro name with appropriate parameters. For example, the sequence of statements necessary to compile, load and execute a Fortran program might be defined as a macro called FORTRAN; this macro might be used with parameters specifying the file name of the source program and the destination of the output. Expansion of a macro and substitution of parameters is performed by the job description interpreter before the job runs; the mechanism is similar to that used in an assembler or a high-level language preprocessor. Most operating systems provide a library of macros for common activities; many also allow users to build up their own libraries to suit individual needs.

    (2) *Control structure.* Job control languages which allow only simple sequences of statements are inadequate for jobs in which the actions to be performed may depend on the outcome of previous steps. Several languages include some form of 'if-statement', so that parts of a job description can be executed only if certain conditions occur. The conditions which may be tested for are generally the result of some previous step; typical examples are the occurrence of an error, the output of a particular message, or the occurrence of a particular value left in a machine register.

    (3) *Parallelism.* Some job control languages include a facility for specifying that various parts of a job may be run in parallel. Such information can be used by the scheduler to initiate a job as a set of processes running in parallel rather than in sequence. The advent of multiprocessor systems, in which real gains can be made by parallelism, will perhaps make this facility more widespread.

11.4 Modern control languages

Modern systems use much more advanced languages in their user interfaces; these combine the facilities already mentioned with increasingly powerful additional facilities. Such languages serve both as command languages, and as job control languages (although the latter function is mainly in the form of files of commands which are then invoked interactively). DCL, as used in VMS, was one of the early developments in this area; others include the UNIX shell (Ritchie *et al.*, 1974), and REXX (Cowlishaw, 1990).

These languages have moved steadily closer to real programming languages; in fact, one of the main uses of REXX is for writing simple 'one-off' programs. They include facilities such as looping and condition constructs, procedures and functions, string manipulation, arithmetic operations, and block structure.

A possible future development lies in pursuing the analogy with high-level programming languages by introducing job control languages which can be compiled or interpreted on any system. This would constitute a significant advance towards machine independence in running jobs; at present the machine independence gained at the programming level is undermined by the different ways jobs must be submitted to different machines. Obstacles to such a development arise from the difficulty of giving widely differing systems the same external interface (Dakin, 1975).

So far as our paper operating system is concerned we shall not attempt to design a particular job control language. Instead we simply remark that any job control language we adopt should contain the features described above, and be designed so as to incorporate those characteristics listed above as desirable from the user's point of view.

11.5 Graphical user interfaces

From the examples given above, it can be seen that the specification of a job, or the choice of the correct commands to be used, is not always completely obvious; there is still a long way to go before many systems can be considered easy to use. This is partly due to the choice of command names and the structure of the user interface language, but it is clear that a different approach is needed. This requirement is even more pressing, given the increasing pervasiveness of microcomputer systems, which often have relatively unsophisticated users.

One possible solution is the *graphical user interface,* or *GUI.* In this kind of user interface, the normal character terminal is replaced by a high resolution graphical screen, together with a normal keyboard and some kind of *pointing device.* The pointing device allows a pointer to be moved around the screen; it may take several forms, of which the most common is the *mouse*. This is used by moving it around a flat surface (e.g. the desktop), while sensors in its base detect the movements and transmit them in coded form to the operating system. The mouse motion is used to move the pointer around the screen; buttons on the mouse provide ways of selecting actions to be performed when the pointer is positioned (for example) over the name of a command.

The power of this kind of interface lies in the fact that many users respond much more readily to pictorial cues rather than to textual ones. However, to consider a GUI merely as a glorified terminal is to do it an injustice; programs can be written to make extensive use of the new interface in a way that would not have been possible with a simple textual one. One example is a program for comparing the contents of two text files; a textual interface can report the differences in only a fairly basic form, whereas a graphical interface can display the two files side by side and draw lines joining portions that are common to both.

On microcomputers, three common interfaces are Microsoft Windows, the IBM OS/2 Workplace Shell, and the Apple Macintosh. Literature on these is changing constantly, so specific references will not be given.

On UNIX systems, the X Window interface is dominant. This interface is particularly interesting because it separates the functions of computation and display, to the extent that a program running on one machine may use a display attached to another, so long as the two machines are connected in some way.

Graphical user interfaces are still under development, and there are many new ideas to come. One of the most important will probably be the concept of *direct manipulation*; this is already present in the OS/2 Workplace Shell, and has been part of the Apple Macintosh for some years in a somewhat reduced form. The basic idea behind direct manipulation is that users move items around the screen in order to make something happen. For example, they can drag a representation of a file to the representation of a printer, and the file will be printed. If the file is dragged to a representation of a program, then the program is invoked, passing the name of the file as a parameter.

11.6 The job pool

We remarked in section 8.4 that jobs awaiting initiation by the scheduler are held in a *job pool*. Each entry in the job pool represents a single job, and contains information about it which is derived from the job description. This information is in fact an encoded form of that contained in the job description, except that in a spooling system all input device names are replaced by the names of the files into which the input has been spooled. The spooling may be performed by the job description interpreter itself, or the interpreter may delegate the task to separate input spoolers (see section 6.6) which it sets in motion by signalling the appropriate semaphores. In either case the interpreter signals to the scheduler whenever a new job pool entry is complete.

The job pool may be structured as a single list or as a number of lists each of which contains jobs with particular characteristics. The latter structure can be a help to the scheduler in choosing which job to run next.

The size of the job pool may prohibit its storage in main memory. However, storage on disk may involve the scheduler in heavy overheads when it comes to search for the best job to run. A possible compromise is to store abbreviated versions of the job pool entries in memory, while the complete entries reside on disk. The abbreviated entries will contain only such information as the scheduler needs to choose the next job; information about input files, for example, can be omitted.

11.7 System messages

The relationship between the user and the operating system depends not only on how easily the user can tell the system what it is required to do, but also on the quality of the information received from it about what it has done. The information supplied by current systems, particularly when job errors have occurred, varies widely in quantity, detail, relevance, and intelligibility. Ideally the degree of detail should depend on the fate of the job; if it terminates successfully then a brief account of the chargeable resources used is probably sufficient, but if it fails then a full statement of the cause is necessary. In all cases system messages should be couched in normal English in such a way as to be easily understood by the general user. All too frequently the user is presented with a mass of apparent gibberish, or, in the case of failure, with a hexadecimal dump!

In a multi-access environment a user should be able to request information about the current state of the system in terms of how many users are logged on, what resources are available, and so on. This information makes it possible to assess what kind of response can be expected and to decide whether or not it is worthwhile continuing the session.

11.8 Passage of a job through the system

Figure 11.1 summarises the stages by which a job progresses from submission to termination through our paper operating system. The solid lines represent the various metamorphoses of the job from job description to job pool entry to

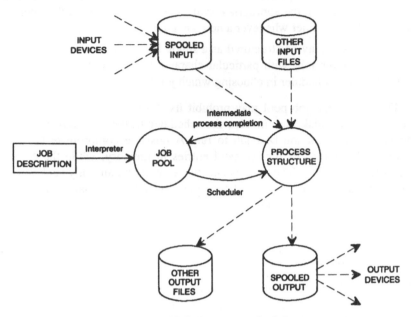

Figure 11.1 Progress of a job

sequence of processes; the broken lines represent the flow of data and programs associated with the job.

If spooling is not employed then the input and output queues can be removed from the diagram and the data transfers shown as being direct to or from the peripheral devices. The circular motion between job pool and process structure is intended to emphasise that it may require the invocation of several processes to execute a single job. Within the process structure itself processes move between the three states blocked, runnable, and running, as previously shown in figure 8.4.

Conclusion

In the last chapter, we completed the construction of our paper operating system by providing it with an interface with the outside world. We also gave an overview of the system by describing the progress of a job from start to finish. It is probably appropriate at this stage to stand back a little and examine what we have achieved.

The purpose of building and describing the paper operating system has been twofold. The primary objective has been to use it as a vehicle for illustrating the mechanisms by which an operating system can fulfil the functions expected of it by its users. The secondary objective has been to support the increasingly popular view that operating systems can become reliable, easily maintained, and relatively error-free only if they exhibit a logically coherent structure. We shall return to this point in a moment.

So far as the primary aim is concerned it is hoped that readers who have reached this point will have a good idea of what operating systems are, what they do, and how they do it. They should understand the nature of the problems posed in operating system design, and the techniques used for overcoming them. In a book as short as this it is of course impossible to give a comprehensive catalogue of all the problems and all the solutions; all one can do is describe those most frequently encountered or adopted. There will inevitably be systems which, because of different user environments or hardware constraints, present problems not covered here; similarly, there will be many systems in which the problems we have mentioned are solved in different ways. However, it is hoped that the material we have presented will provide an adequate basis from which readers can broaden their knowledge according to their interests. The ground should be sufficiently well prepared for seeds from elsewhere to flourish.

The second point mentioned above, concerning the logical structure of operating systems, is one which merits further discussion. We have constructed on paper a system which is neatly layered, with each layer dependent only on the layers below it. However, it must be admitted that when we constructed the system the dice were loaded in our favour. First, we were not distracted by the problems of working in a large team, and second, we were not obliged by customer demand to add new features after the initial design stage. Third, and perhaps most important, we did not have to make the system work on a real

machine. The question must therefore be asked: how far is it possible to trans-
late the structure of the paper operating system into real life?

The first two obstacles – those of large project teams and changing specifications – can be avoided by judicious management. The third obstacle – that
of intransigent machine architecture – is more difficult to overcome, particularly in the short term. Machine architecture impinges on the system at many
levels, but the areas most directly influenced are interrupt handling, I/O, and
memory protection. It is worth looking at each of these in turn.

As indicated in chapter 4, the complexity of the interrupt handler can vary
greatly according to the amount of help given by the hardware. This help is
particularly important in interrupt identification and in the determination of
priorities. For example the VAX, which provides a hardware priority mechanism in which devices may be assigned to any one of 16 levels, gives more help
than the IBM 370 series, in which priority is largely predetermined and can be
modified only partially by selective software masking. Both machines do
however provide adequate information for the source and nature of an interrupt
to be readily determined.

The framework for I/O handling established in chapter 6 can become
severely distorted by the constraints of a particular I/O architecture. The
framework is well suited to architectures based on a simple bus system, but
may have to be modified in cases (such as the IBM 370) involving a hierarchy
of channels, control units, and devices. Terminals, because of their special
control function, are treated as special cases in most systems. On some systems, for example, terminal buffers are allocated from space belonging to the
operating system, rather than (as is the case for some other devices) from space
belonging to individual user processes. The reason for this stems from the fact
that a process which is performing I/O cannot be moved to secondary memory
as its buffers would then be overwritten by whichever process replaced it.
Since terminal buffers are always potentially in use it follows that if they were
allocated from user space the corresponding user processes would have to be
resident permanently in main memory.

The architectural feature which most seriously affects the structure of an
operating system is probably the mechanism for memory protection and management. The total realisation of the layered structure of our paper operating
system implies the existence of a protection system that can be made to mirror
it. It seems that the segment, being the logical unit of address space, should be
the natural unit for protection, and that what is required is the ability to create
an arbitrary number of protection domains. One machine which departs far
from the ideal is the IBM 370. Here protection is applied not to segments but
to 2K or 4K byte blocks of physical memory; the confusion between logical
and physical divisions of memory is made even worse by allowing the page
field of an address to overflow into the segment field. Several machines apply

protection to segments, but very few have more than two or three protection domains. The most common arrangement is the two-domain 'supervisor-user' system, typified by the IBM 370 and many microprocessors. Multiple domains exist in the DEC VAX (four), the Intel 80486 (four) and the ICL 2900 series (sixteen), but besides being of a limited number they tend to carry a high operational overhead in most cases. The problems of implementing multiple domains at low cost are by no means yet solved; the use of capabilities as described in chapter 9 is perhaps the most promising approach. However, despite the deficiencies of current architectures, we can expect that new protection mechanisms will soon provide the means for facilitating layered system structure. In the meantime we can regard structure as a legitimate objective while lacking the means to enforce it.

What other developments can be expected? Crystal ball gazing is a hazardous occupation in such a rapidly changing field, but we shall indulge in it briefly at the risk of being proved wrong by events. Short-term developments are likely to be concentrated on improving the reliability of operating systems, on making them more easily portable between different machines (one example of this is UNIX), and on making them easier to use by means of more powerful and flexible user interfaces (for example, the graphical user interfaces mentioned in chapter 11). In the longer term the two factors which will most influence the nature and role of operating systems are the rapid development of extremely powerful and sophisticated microprocessors (the Intel 80486 and the DEC Alpha are good examples of the current state of the art in this area), and the provision of improved communications and networking facilities both at the local area and wide area levels.

Microprocessors already offer a new form of processing power – small discrete units of very low cost, in contrast to the large, monolithic, expensive units of the last few decades – and great advances are still being made. The challenge they present is to exploit this power to the best advantage. One trend is already apparent: the dispersal of computing facilities to the places where they are most needed, rather than their concentration in a central location. The rapidly decreasing cost of processors, memory, and secondary storage devices has made it economically feasible to dedicate a complete computing system to a single application, be it payroll, process control, teaching, home budgeting, or whatever. Resource allocation, which is one of the chief functions of the traditional mainframe operating system, becomes trivial in such a dedicated system, since the resources required are always available. It is interesting to note, however, that such is the power of the latest microprocessor systems that they have become single-user, multi-tasking systems which are capable of performing several tasks for the user at the same time; we are thus moving back into the area of larger scale operating systems, albeit from a slightly different viewpoint.

Dedicated systems may be completely independent, or they may be linked by means of data transmission lines. In the latter case, information stored at one site can be transmitted for use at another, or work which is beyond the capacity of a single installation can be passed elsewhere for processing. The ability to link semi-independent installations into a large network gives the potential of delivering enormous computing power and information accessing capability to widely dispersed individuals or groups. Such networks now exist in many countries, and most of them are interconnected. The function of an operating system in such an environment includes message transmission and validation, load sharing, and the maintenance of the consistency of information which may be held in several forms at different sites.

Another possible development, in areas where large amounts of concentrated computing power are still required, is to replace the mainframe CPU by a collection of interconnected processors. Such systems range from small groups of tightly coupled machines sharing a common set of disks and files (for example DEC's VAXCluster) to larger groups of microprocessors connected by lower cost networks, each perhaps having a small amount of local secondary storage as well as access to a common, larger, storage system. A natural progression is to have a system in which each process has its own processor, thus increasing the parallelism in the system and eliminating the need for process switching. Another advantage is the potential increase in reliability which comes from the replication of processors. There are, however, several problems which must be overcome before such a system can be realised. One of the principal ones concerns memory organisation: should each processor have its own private memory, should they all share a common memory, or should there be a combination of the two? Common memory brings problems of contention for access, while private memories imply a requirement for easy transmission of data between them. Mixed memory requires solutions to both types of problem, as well as that of devising and implementing an appropriate address map. Other architectural problems are the direction of external interrupts to the appropriate processor, and the provision of a mechanism for communication between processors. At the operating system level there are problems concerned with the recognition of potential parallelism, the allocation of processes to processors, communication between processes which may share no common memory, the sharing of resources, and error detection and recovery. All these problems are being vigorously tackled, and one can expect viable multi-microprocessor systems to become a reality within the next few years; already good progress has been made with systems built round the Transputer (May and Shepherd, 1985).

Finally, we would urge the reader not to regard this book as in any way a definitive study of operating systems. There are many excellent papers and books which will give fresh insight to the material covered here, or which will introduce the reader to new ground. It is hoped that the references given at the end of the book will provide an adequate starting point.

Appendix: Monitors

The general structure of a monitor (Hoare, 1974), using a Pascal-like syntax, is

    var *m*: *monitor*;
    begin
        declaration of local variables representing the shared object;
        declaration of procedures accessing the local variables;
        initialisation of local variables
    end

The local variables are inaccessible outside the monitor; after initialisation they may be operated on only by the monitor procedures themselves. To prevent simultaneous manipulation of the local variables by several processes the monitor procedures are implemented as mutually exclusive critical sections. Mutual exclusion is guaranteed by the compiler, which generates appropriate synchronisation operations (such as *wait* and *signal* operations on semaphores) in the compiled program. (For the reader familiar with abstract data types, a monitor can be regarded as an abstract data object which can safely be shared by several processes.)

Although mutual exclusion of monitor procedures is guaranteed by the compiler, other forms of synchronisation remain the responsibility of the programmer. The synchronisation operations suggested by Hoare, and adopted in most monitor implementations, are not *wait* and *signal* operations on semaphores, but similar operations on objects called *conditions*. Like a semaphore, a condition has two operations which can be applied to it – one is used to delay a process and the other to resume it. We shall refer to these operations as *cwait* and *csignal* respectively to distinguish them from the *wait* and *signal* operations on semaphores.

The definitions of *cwait* and *csignal* are

cwait (*condition*):	suspend execution of the calling process
csignal (*condition*):	resume execution of some process suspended after a *cwait* on the same condition. If there are several such processes, choose one of them; if there is no such process, do nothing

The *cwait* operation releases exclusion on the monitor – otherwise no other process would be able to enter the monitor to perform a *csignal*. Similarly, *csignal* releases exclusion, handing it to the process which is resumed. The resumed process must therefore be permitted to run before any other process can enter the monitor.

Although conditions and semaphores are used for similar purposes, the following differences are significant.

(a) A condition, unlike a semaphore, does not have a value. It can be thought of as a queue to which a process is added on performing *cwait* and from which it is removed when some other process performs a *csignal*.

(b) A *cwait* operation always causes the executing process to be delayed. This contrasts with the *wait* operation, which causes delay only when the semaphore value is zero.

(c) A *csignal* operation has an effect only if a process is suspended on the same condition. A *signal* operation, on the other hand, always has an effect – that of incrementing the semaphore value. Thus *signal* operations are 'remembered' (in the value of the semaphore), whereas *csignal* operations are not.

As an example of the use of conditions for synchronisation, we give details of the buffer monitor referred to in section 3.4

```
var buffer: monitor;
begin
    var B: array[0...N - 1] of item;      { space for N items }
        nextin, nextout: 0...N - 1;       {buffer pointers }
        nonfull, nonempty: condition;     { for synchronisation }
        count: 0...N;                     { number of items in buffer }

    procedure deposit(x: item);
    begin
        if count = N then cwait(nonfull);     { avoid overflow }
        B[nextin] := x;
        nextin := (nextin + 1) mod N;
        count : = count + 1;               { one more item in buffer }
        csignal(nonempty)                  { resume any waiting }
                                           { consumer }
    end;
```

```
procedure extract(var x: item);
begin
    if count = 0 then cwait(nonempty);    { avoid underflow }
    x := B[nextout];
    nextout : = (nextout + 1) mod N;
    count := count - 1;                   { one fewer item in buffer }
    csignal(nonfull)                      { resume any waiting }
                                          { producer }
end;

nextin := 0;
nextout := 0;
count : = 0                               { buffer initially empty }
end
```

References

Advanced Micro Devices (1988), *Am29000 Streamlined Instruction Processor*, Advanced Micro Devices, Sunnyvale, California

Alagic, S., and Arbib, M.A. (1978), *The Design of Well-Structured and Correct Programs*, Springer-Verlag, New York

Andrews, G.R., and Schneider, F.B. (1983), Concepts and notations for concurrent programming, *Computing Surveys*, **15**, 3-13

Avizienis, A. (1977), Fault-tolerant Computing: Progress, Problems and Prospects, *Proc. IFIPS 77*, North-Holland, Amsterdam, 405

Bach, M.J. (1986), *The Design of the UNIX Operating System*, Prentice Hall, Englewood Cliffs, New Jersey

Baron, R.J., and Higbie, L. (1992), *Computer Architecture*, Addison-Wesley, Reading, Massachusetts

Ben-Ari, M. (1982), *Principles of Concurrent Programming*, Prentice Hall, Englewood Cliffs, New Jersey

Brooks, F.P. (1975), *The Mythical Man-Month*, Addison-Wesley, Reading, Massachusetts

Buckle, J.K. (1978), *The ICL 2900 Series*, Macmillan, London and Basingstoke

Cheriton, D.R., Malcolm, M.A., Melen, L.S., and Sager, G.R. (1979), Thoth, a portable real-time operating system, *Comm. ACM*, **22**, 2, 105-115

Coffman, E.G., Elphick, M., and Shoshani, A. (1971), System deadlocks, *Computing Surveys*, **3**, 2, 67-78

Coffman, E.G., and Kleinrock, L. (1968), Computer scheduling methods and their countermeasures, *Proc. AFIPS Spring Joint Computer Conference*, **32**, 11-21

Courtois, P.J., Heymans, R., and Parnas, D.L. (1971), Concurrent control with "readers" and "writers", *Comm. ACM*, **14**, 10, 667-668

Cowlishaw, M.F. (1990), *The REXX Language*, Second Edition, Prentice Hall, Englewood Cliffs, New Jersey

Custer, H. (1993), *Inside Windows NT*, Microsoft Press, Redmond, Washington

Corbató, F.J., Merwin-Dagget, M., and Daley, R.C. (1962), An experimental time sharing system, *Proc. AFIPS Spring Joint Computer Conference*, **21**, 335-344

Dahl, O.J., Dijkstra, E.W., and Hoare, C.A.R. (1972), *Structured Programming*, Academic Press, London and New York

Dakin, R.J. (1975), A general control language: structure and translation, *Computer Journal*, **18**, 324-332

Daley, R.C., and Dennis, J.B. (1968), Virtual memory, processes, and sharing in MULTICS, *Comm. ACM*, **11**, 5, 306-312

Deitel, H.M. (1990), *Operating Systems*, 2nd edition, Addison-Wesley, Reading, Massachusetts

Deitel, H.M. and Kogan, M.S. (1992), *The Design of OS/2*, Addison-Wesley, Reading, Massachusetts

Denning, P.J. (1968), The working set model for program behaviour, *Comm. ACM*, **11**, 5, 323-333

Denning, P.J. (1970), Virtual memory, *Computing Surveys*, **2**, 3, 153-189

Denning, P.J. (1976), Fault-tolerant operating systems, *Computing Surveys*, **8**, 4, 359-389

Denning, P.J. (1980), Working Sets – Past and Present, *IEEE Trans. Software Engineering*, **6**, 1, 64-84

Digital Equipment Corporation (1975), *PDP-11 Processor Handbook*, Digital Equipment Corporation, Maynard, Massachusetts

Dijkstra, E.W. (1965), Co-operating sequential processes, in *Programming Languages* (ed. F. Genuys), Academic Press, New York (1968)

Dijkstra, E.W. (1968), The structure of the T.H.E. multiprogramming system, *Comm. ACM*, **11**, 5, 341-346

Dijkstra, E.W. (1976), *A Discipline of Programming*, Prentice Hall, Englewood Cliffs, New Jersey

Duncan, R. (ed.) (1988), *The MS-DOS Encyclopedia*, Microsoft Press, Redmond, Washington

Duncan, R. (1990), Design goals and implementation of the new High Performance File System, *Microsoft Systems Journal*, **4**, 5, 1-13

Ellis, M., and Stroustrup, B. (1990), *The Annotated C++ Reference Manual*, Addison-Wesley, Reading, Massachusetts

England, D .M. (1974), The capability concept mechanism and structure in System-250, *IRIA International Workshop on Protection in Operating Systems*, Rocquencourt, 63-82

Evans, D.C., and Leclerc, J.Y. (1967), Address mapping and the control of access in an interactive computer, *Proc. AFIPS Spring Joint Computer Conference*, **30**, 23-32

Fabry, S. (1974), Capability based addressing, *Comm. ACM*, **17**, 7, 403-12

Fagan, M.E. (1976), Design and code inspections to reduce errors in program development, *IBM Systems Journal*, **15**, 3, 182-211

Floyd, R.W. (1967), Assigning meanings to programs, *Proc. Symposium in Applied Maths*, **19**, American Mathematical Society

Folk, M.J., and Zoellick, B. (1987), *File Structures – A Conceptual Toolkit*, Addison-Wesley, Reading, Massachusetts

Goldenberg, R.E. and Kenah, L.J. (1991), *VAX/VMS Internals and Data Structures*, Digital Press, Bedford, Massachusetts

Graham, R.M. (1968), Protection in an information processing utility, *Comm. ACM*, **11**, 5, 365-369

Habermann, A.N. (1969), Prevention of system deadlocks, *Comm. ACM*, **12**, 7, 373-386

Habermann, A.N. (1972), Synchronisation of communicating processes, *Comm. ACM*, **15**, 3, 171-176

Hansen, P.B. (1970), The nucleus of a multiprogramming system, *Comm. ACM*, **13**, 4, 238-241, 250

Hansen, P.B. (1975), The programming language Concurrent Pascal, *IEEE Trans. Software Engineering*, **1**, 2, 199-207

Hantler, S.L., and King, J.C. (1976), An introduction to proving the correctness of programs, *Computing Surveys*, **8**, 3, 331-353

Hartley, D.F. (1970), Management software in multiple-access systems, *Bulletin of the I.M.A.*, **6**, 11-13

Havender, J.W. (1968), Avoiding deadlock in multitasking systems, *IBM Systems Journal*, **7**, 2, 74-84

Hayes, I. (1987), *Specification Case Studies*, Prentice Hall, Englewood Cliffs, New Jersey

Hoare, C.A.R. (1972), Proof of correctness of data representation, *Acta Informatica*, **1**, 271-281

Hoare, C.A.R. (1974), Monitors: an operating system structuring concept, *Comm. ACM*, **17**, 10, 549-557

Holt, R.C., and Cordy, J.R. (1988), The Turing Programming Language, *Comm. ACM*, **31**, 12, 1410-1423

Horning, J., Lauer, H.C., Melliar-Smith, P.M., and Randell, B. (1974), A program structure for error detection and recovery, in *Lecture Notes in Computer Science*, **16**, Springer-Verlag, New York

Huxtable, D.H.R. and Pinkerton, J.M.M. (1977), The hardware-software interface of the ICL 2900 range of computers, *Computer Journal*, **20**, 290-295

IBM Corporation, *IBM System/360 Operating System Concepts and Facilities*, Manual C28-6535

IBM Corporation, *IBM System/370 Principles of Operation*, Manual GA22-7000

IBM Corporation, *IBM System/370 Extended Architecture*, Manual SA22-7085

ICL (1969), *Operating Systems George 3 and 4*, Manual 4169

Intel Corporation, *i486 Processor Programmer's Reference Manual*, Manual 240486, Intel Corporation, Santa Clara, California

ISO (1988), *Information Processing – Volume and file structure of CD-ROM for information interchange*, ISO 9660:1988 (E), International Standards Organisation

Keedy, J.L. (1976), The management and technological approach to the design of System B, *Proc. 7th Australian Computer Conf.*, Perth, 997-1013

Kernighan, B.W., and Ritchie, D.M. (1988), *The C Programming Language*, 2nd edition, Prentice Hall, Englewood Cliffs, New Jersey

Knuth, D.E. (1973), *The Art of Computer Programming; Volume 1: Fundamental algorithms*, 2nd edition, Addison-Wesley, Reading, Massachusetts

Lampson, B.W., and Redell, D. (1980), Experience with processes and monitors in Mesa, *Comm. ACM*, **23**, 2, 105-117

Leffler, S.J., McKusick, M.K., Karels, M.J., and Quarterman, J.S. (1989), *The Design and Implementation of the 4.3BSD UNIX Operating System*, Addison-Wesley, Reading, Massachusetts

Leonard, T. (ed) (1987), *VAX Architecture Reference Manual*, Digital Press, Bedford, Massachusetts

Lister, A.M. (1974), Validation of systems of parallel processes, *Computer Journal*, **17**, 148-151

Martin, J. (1977), *Computer Data-Base Organisation*, 2nd ed., Prentice Hall, Englewood Cliffs, New Jersey

May, D., and Shepherd, R. (1985), Occam and the Transputer, in *Concurrent Languages in Distributed Systems*, North-Holland, Amsterdam

McCoy, K. (1990), *VMS File System Internals*, Digital Press, Bedford, Massachusetts

McKell, L.J., Hansen, J.V., and Heitger, L.E. (1979), Charging for Computer Resources, *Computing Surveys*, **11**, 2, 105-120

Minoura, T. (1982), Deadlock Avoidance Revisited, *Journal of the ACM*, **24**, 4, 1023-1048

Morris, D., and Ibbett, R.N. (1979), *The MU5 Computer System*, Macmillan, London and Basingstoke

Nelson, V.P. (1990), Fault tolerant computing: fundamental concepts, *Computer*, **23**, 7, 19-25

Organick, E.I. (1972), *The Multics System*, MIT Press, Cambridge, Massachusetts

Parmelee, R.P., Peterson, T.I., Tillman, C.C., and Hatfield, D.J. (1972), Virtual storage and virtual machine concepts, *IBM Systems Journal*, **11**, 2, 99-130

QIC, Inc., *QIC Development Standards* (several), Quarter Inch Drive Standards, Inc., Santa Barbara, California

Randell, B. (1975), System structure for software fault tolerance, *IEEE Trans. Software Engineering*, **1**, 2, 220-232

Randell, B., Lee, P.A., and Treleaven, P.C. (1978), Reliability issues in computing system design, *Computing Surveys*, **10**, 2, 123-165

Rees, D.J. (1975), The EMAS Director, *Computer Journal*, **18**, 122-130

Richards, M., and Whitby-Strevens, C. (1979), *BCPL – the language and its compiler*, Cambridge University Press, Cambridge, England

Ritchie, D.M., and Thompson, K. (1974), The UNIX time-sharing system, *Comm. ACM*, **17**, 7, 365-375

Saltzer, J.H. (1974), Protection and the Control of Information Sharing in Multics, *Comm. ACM*, **17**, 7, 388-402

Saltzer, J.H., and Schroeder, M.D. (1975), The Protection of Information in Computer Systems, *Proc. IEEE*, **63**, 9, 1278-1308

Sauer, C.H., and Chandy, K.M. (1981), *Computer Systems Performance Modeling*, Prentice Hall, Englewood Cliffs, New Jersey

Schroeder, M.D., and Saltzer, J.H. (1972), A hardware architecture for implementing protection rings, *Comm. ACM*, **15**, 3, 157-170

Seawright, L.H., and MacKinnon, R.A. (1979), VM/370 – A Study of Multiplicity and Usefulness, *IBM Systems Journal*, **18**, 1, 4-17

Shooman, M.L. (1984), *Software Engineering: Reliability, Development and Management*, McGraw-Hill, New York

Silberschatz, A., Peterson, J.L., and Galvin, P.B. (1991), *Operating System Concepts*, 3rd edition, Addison-Wesley, Reading, Massachusetts

Tanenbaum, A.S. (1987), *Operating Systems: Design and Implementation*, Prentice Hall, Englewood Cliffs, New Jersey

Thompson, K. (1978), UNIX Implementation, *Bell System Technical Jour nal*, **57,6**, Part 2

Sites, R.L. (1993), Alpha AXP Architecture, *Comm. ACM*, **36**, 2, 33-44

Wegner, P., and Smolka, S.A. (1983), Processes, Tasks and Monitors: A Comparative Study of Concurrent Programming Primitives, *IEEE Trans. Software Engineering*, **9**, 4, 446-462

Welsh, J., and Bustard, D.W. (1979), Pascal-plus – another language for modular multiprogramming, *Software – Practice and Experience*, **9**, 947-957

Whitfield, H., and Wight, A.S. (1973), EMAS – The Edinburgh Multi Access System, *Computer Journal*, **16**, 331-346

Wiener, R.S., and Pinson, L.J. (1988), *An Introduction to Object-Oriented Programming*, Addison-Wesley, Reading, Massachusetts

Wight, A.S. (1975), The EMAS Archiving Program, *Computer Journal*, **18**, 131-134

Williams, R.K. (1972), System 250 basic concepts, *Proc. Conference on Computers Systems and Technology*, I.E.R.E. Conference Proceedings number 25, 157-168

Wirth, N. (1971), Program development by stepwise refinement, *Comm. ACM*, **14**, 4, 221-227

Wirth, N. (1977), Modula: a language for modular multiprogramming, *Software – Practice and Experience*, **7**, 3-36

Wirth, N. (1985), *Programming in Modula-2*, 3rd ed., Springer-Verlag, Heidelberg,

Wulf, W.A., Russell, D.B., and Habermann, A.N. (1971), BLISS: a language for systems programming, *Comm. ACM*, **14**, 12, 780-790

Wulf, W.A. (1975), Reliable hardware-software architecture, *IEEE Trans. Software Engineering*, **1**, 2, 233-240

Yourdon, E., and Constantine, L.L. (1979), *Structured Design*, Prentice Hall, Englewood Cliffs, New Jersey

Yourdon, E. (1989), *Modern Structured Analysis*, Prentice Hall, Englewood Cliffs, New Jersey

Index